PACEMAKER® PRACTICAL ENGLISH SERIES

CAPITALIZATION AND PUNCTUATION MAKE SENSE

Arlene G. Clarke
Marlene B. Clarke

A PACEMAKER® BOOK

Fearon Education
Belmont, California

Simon & Schuster Supplementary Education Group

Pacemaker® Practical English Series

Grammar Makes Sense
Capitalization and Punctuation Make Sense
Writing Makes Sense
Spelling Makes Sense
Vocabulary Makes Sense

ISBN 0-8224-5102-6

Printed in the United States of America

1. 9 8 7 6 5 4

CONTENTS

Capitalization

First word in a sentence 1
Personal pronoun *I* 3
Names and initials of people 5
Titles of people 7
Names of relatives 9
Names of days 10
Names of months 12
Writing Activity 1 14
Names of holidays 16
Names of streets and highways 17
Names of cities and towns 19
Names of states, countries, and continents 22
Names of mountains and bodies of water 24
Writing Activity 2 26
Abbreviations 28
Titles of works 31
Other proper nouns 34
Proper adjectives 36
Direct quotations 37
Greetings and closings in letters 39
Outlines 40
Writing Activity 3 42

Punctuation

Punctuation marks at the ends of sentences 43
Periods with abbreviations 45
Periods after initials 47

Commas in dates 49
Commas in place names 51
Writing Activity 4 54
Commas in compound sentences 56
Commas in series 60
Commas after introductory phrases and clauses 63
Commas with nouns of address 67
Commas with appositives 69
Writing Activity 5 72
Commas or exclamation points with interjections 74
Commas after greetings in friendly letters 76
Commas after closings in friendly letters and business letters 77
Writing Activity 6 78
Quotation marks with direct quotations 79
Commas with direct quotations 83
End punctuation with direct quotations 87
Writing Activity 7 90
Quotation marks with titles of works 92
Underlines with titles of works 94
Apostrophes in contractions 96
Apostrophes in possessive nouns 99
Colons after greetings in business letters 103
Writing Activity 8 104
Colons in expressions of time 106
Hyphens in numbers and fractions 107
Posttest 109
Reference Guide 111

CAPITALIZING

First word in a sentence

If you need help with capitalizing the first word in a sentence, turn to Capitalization Rule 1 on page 119.

PRECHECK. In each sentence below, find the word that should be capitalized. Then write the word correctly on the line next to the sentence. Check your answers at the bottom of the page.

1. about ten footballs are used in a pro football game. ____________
2. yo-yos were originally weapons, not toys. ____________
3. in some places, men woo women by blowing smoke at them. ____________
4. cockroaches clean themselves after coming near people. ____________
5. coin-operated vending machines are about 2,000 years old. ____________

Number right: _____ *If less than 5, review the rule in the Reference Guide.*

In each sentence below, find the word that should be capitalized. Then write the word correctly on the line next to the sentence.

1. a young sailor threw a pie at an officer. ____________
2. it was a chocolate cream pie. ____________
3. the sailor was put on trial for assault. ____________
4. television comic Soupy Sales testified for him. ____________
5. sales had had 19,253 pies thrown in his face. ____________
6. he did not consider it assault. ____________
7. but the sailor was still found guilty. ____________

ANSWERS 1. About 2. Yo-yos 3. In 4. Cockroaches 5. Coin-operated

CAPITALIZING

First word in a sentence

If you need help with capitalizing the first word in a sentence, turn to Capitalization Rule 1 on page 119.

On the lines below, rewrite the paragraph given on the right. Make sure that the first word in each sentence starts with a capital letter.

few people know about one of our secret weapons in World War II. it was bats. the army caught 30 million bats. it put a little bomb on each bat. the army was going to release the bats in enemy cities. then the bats would fly to the dark corners and attics of buildings. when the bat bombs went off, the buildings would burn down. the army spent $2 million on the plan. but the plan was never used. maybe the army decided the plan was too batty after all.

CAPITALIZING

Personal pronoun *I*

If you need help with capitalizing the personal pronoun I, *turn to Capitalization Rule 2 on page 119.*

Rewrite each sentence below. Make sure you capitalize the personal pronoun *I*.

1. For years, i wanted a car.

___

2. To earn the money, i worked after school.

___

3. At last, i had $1,500.

___

4. At Honest Joe's Used Cars, i saw the car of my dreams.

___

5. The red sports car was just what i wanted.

___

6. i knew i would enjoy driving it.

___

7. So i offered Honest Joe $1,000.

___

8. When he turned me down, i offered $1,200.

___

9. He accepted, and i was very happy.

___

10. Now i had enough money left over to make the car run.

___

CAPITALIZING

Personal pronoun *I*

If you need help with capitalizing the personal pronoun I, *turn to Capitalization Rule 2 on page 119.*

On the lines below, rewrite the paragraph given on the right. Replace the * with the personal pronoun *I*.**

All my life, *** wanted to be a television star. One day *** saw a Help Wanted sign outside the television studio. *** decided to apply for the job. After *** went in, *** saw the station manager. He asked me if *** could run errands, move props, and answer the phone. *** said that *** could since *** had been doing that for my mother for years. So he said *** was hired.

CAPITALIZING

Names and initials of people
Titles of people
Names of relatives

If you need help with capitalizing names and initials of people, titles of people, and names of relatives, turn to Capitalization Rules 3, 4, and 5 on page 119.

PRECHECK. In the sentences below, find the people's names, initials, and titles that should be capitalized. Write them correctly on the lines next to the sentences. Check your answers at the bottom of the page.

1. A paratrooper named his children ripcord and canopy. ____________________
2. Ben Casey's boss was dr. zorba. ____________________
3. In The Wizard of Oz, Dorothy's aunt is auntie em. ____________________
4. 2001 was written by arthur c. clarke. ____________________
5. Some say president lincoln haunts the White House. ____________________

Number right: _____ *If less than 5, review the rules in the Reference Guide.*

CAPITALIZING

Names and initials of people

In the sentences below, find the people's names and initials that should be capitalized. Then write them correctly on the lines next to the sentences.

1. At the age of 93, g. b. shaw wrote a play. ____________________
2. Englishman charlie roberts created square tomatoes. ____________________
3. Pitcher bobo newsom was traded 16 times. ____________________
4. In 1978, herb robbins sponsored a worm-eating contest. ____________________
5. A state was once named after benjamin franklin. ____________________
6. World War II carrier pigeon g. i. joe saved many lives. ____________________
7. Mr. j. c. dithers is Dagwood's boss. ____________________

ANSWERS 1. Ripcord, Canopy 2. Dr. Zorba 3. Auntie Em 4. Arthur C. Clarke 5. President Lincoln

CAPITALIZING

Names and initials of people

If you need help with capitalizing names and initials of people, turn to Capitalization Rule 3 on page 119.

On the lines below, rewrite the paragraph given on the right. Make sure that you capitalize people's names and initials.

Many famous people have had interesting pets. British statesman winston churchill had his cat attend cabinet meetings. When he was at war, robert e. lee wanted a cat for company. So famous was gerald r. ford's dog, Patsy, that many people asked for her paw print. President woodrow wilson had sheep to help keep the White House lawn short. President calvin coolidge had a pet raccoon, Rebecca. One of teddy roosevelt's daughters, alice, had a snake she named Emily Spinach. During abraham lincoln's term in office, his son tad had a pet turkey named Jack. As you can see, many animals have lived in the White House—and not all of them have been presidents.

CAPITALIZING

Titles of people

If you need help with capitalizing titles of people, turn to Capitalization Rule 4 on page 119.

In each sentence below, find the title that should be capitalized. Then write the title correctly on the line next to the sentence.

1. Peter Sellers played the bumbling inspector Clouseau. __________
2. In her hat, queen Marie Antoinette put potato flowers. __________
3. A famous monster was created by dr. Frankenstein. __________
4. Dickens made mr. Ebenezer Scrooge famous. __________
5. His men called general Custer "Curly" and "Ringlets." __________
6. Millionaire mrs. Hetty Green ate only cold oatmeal. __________
7. In 1953, senator Wayne Morse spoke for over 22 hours straight. __________
8. In the Tower of London, king Henry I kept a polar bear. __________

Rewrite each sentence below. Be sure to capitalize titles of people.

1. Frequently, admiral Horatio Nelson was seasick.

   ____

2. During the war, princess Elizabeth worked as a mechanic.

   ____

3. In 1924, dr. Spock rowed in the Olympics.

   ____

4. Napoleon's followers called him "corporal Violet."

   ____

5. A ten-ton ball of string is owned by mr. Francis Johnson.

   ____

CAPITALIZING

Titles of people

If you need help with capitalizing titles of people, turn to Capitalization Rule 4 on page 119.

On the lines below, rewrite the paragraph given on the right. Be sure to capitalize titles of people.

Many comic strips and television shows are about army life. For years, people have laughed at private Beetle Bailey, lieutenant Fuzz, and general Halftrack. On television, we have enjoyed watching sergeant Bilko and colonel J. T. Hall. On Hogan's Heroes, we saw colonel Hogan outsmart sergeant Schultz and commandant Klink. M*A*S*H has shown us dr. Pierce playing tricks on major Burns and nurse Houlihan. And who can forget corporal Klinger, who is always dressed in the latest fashion? On Star Trek, we saw the army of the future. At first captain Pike and then captain Kirk defeated the forces of evil with the help of the clever mr. Spock and the skillful dr. McCoy. More recently, we have watched private Benjamin survive the army—and the army survive her.

CAPITALIZING

Names of relatives

If you need help with capitalizing names of relatives, *turn to Capitalization Rule 5 on page 119.*

In each sentence below, find the relative's name that should be capitalized. Then write the name correctly on the line next to the sentence.

1. Comic Milton Berle was called uncle miltie. ______
2. Will Geer was grandpa walton. ______
3. Every mother hears, "But, mom, all my friends are going!" ______
4. Every father hears, "May I borrow the car, dad?" ______
5. My favorite aunt is aunt hill. ______
6. These cookies grandma baked taste almost homemade. ______
7. Little Orphan Annie is adopted by daddy warbucks. ______

Rewrite the sentences below. Be sure to capitalize names of relatives.

1. In <u>Tom Sawyer</u>, brother sid is a goody-goody.

   ______

2. Batman's aunt is aunt harriet.

   ______

3. In the 1940s, many men found out they had an uncle sam.

   ______

4. "Please turn down the stereo, mom. I'm trying to study."

   ______

5. Irene Ryan played granny on <u>The Beverly Hillbillies</u>.

   ______

CAPITALIZING

Names of days
Names of months

If you need help with capitalizing names of days and months, turn to Capitalization Rules 6 and 7 on page 119.

PRECHECK. In each sentence below, find the name of the day or month that should be capitalized. Then write the name correctly on the line next to the sentence. Check your answers at the bottom of the page.

1. Bears are born in the last week of january. ______
2. The poem says, "thursday's child has far to go." ______
3. The last Beatles concert was on august 29, 1966. ______
4. Our ancestors named monday after the moon. ______
5. The emerald is the birthstone of people born in may. ______

Number right: ____ *If less than 5, review the rules in the Reference Guide.*

CAPITALIZING

Names of days

In each sentence below, find the name of the day that should be capitalized. Then write the name correctly on the line next to the sentence.

1. On sunday night, Carter set his alarm for 6:30. ______
2. On monday morning, he jumped up when the alarm went off. ______
3. When he went to bed on tuesday, he set the alarm for 7:00. ______
4. At 7:30 on wednesday morning, he rolled out of bed. ______
5. Carter set his alarm for 7:30 each thursday night. ______
6. At 8:00 on friday morning, he dragged himself out of bed. ______
7. On saturday, he didn't get up until noon. ______

ANSWERS 1. January 2. Thursday's 3. August 4. Monday 5. May

CAPITALIZING

Names of days

If you need help with capitalizing names of days, turn to Capitalization Rule 6 on page 119.

Here is a page from Darryl's calendar. Use it to help you fill in the days of the week that belong in the paragraph below.

MAY						
SUNDAY	MONDAY	TUESDAY	WEDNESDAY	THURSDAY	FRIDAY	SATURDAY
1	2	3 job interview	4	5	6	7 call Carla
8 picnic	9	10 get car fixed	11 dentist	12 pick up car	13	14
15	16 go to library	17	18	19	20	21
22	23 start job	24	25	26	27 history report due	28
29	30 library books due	31				

Darryl had a very busy month. On the first ____________________ of the month, he had a job interview. Four days later, on ____________________, he called Carla to tell her he had a job that would start on ____________________, May 23. They decided to go on a picnic on ____________________ to celebrate.

Now that he had a job, Darryl decided to get his car fixed on ____________________. The car was not ready on ____________________, so he had to take the bus to the dentist. He picked the car up on ____________________.

Darryl wanted to begin his history report before his job started. On ____________________, May 16, he went to the library. The report was due on ____________________, May 27. He could keep the books until the following ____________________. May was a busy month, but Darryl was able to fit everything in.

CAPITALIZING

Names of months

If you need help with capitalizing names of months, turn to Capitalization Rule 7 on page 119.

In each sentence below, find the name of the month that should be capitalized. Then write the name correctly on the line next to the sentence.

1. Cigarette ads were taken off TV on january 3, 1971. ________________
2. Blue jeans were first introduced in may 1873. ________________
3. Hank Aaron broke Ruth's lifetime home-run record on april 8, 1974. ________________
4. A library book taken out in 1823 was returned in december 1968. ________________
5. Michael Jackson was born on august 29, 1958. ________________
6. Bobby Fischer became the world chess champion on september 1, 1972. ________________
7. President Kennedy was shot on november 22, 1963. ________________
8. Oregon became our thirty-third state on february 14, 1859. ________________
9. The U.S. Constitution went into effect in march 1789. ________________
10. In october 1942, the Queen Mary rammed and sank a British cruiser. ________________

The following paragraph is missing the names of months. Use the months listed to complete the paragraph. Be sure to capitalize the names of the months.

january
march
june
august
july
april

The names of the months have meanings. Janus, a two-faced god, gave his name to ________________. The month ________________ is named after Mars. Since flowers open in spring, the word *aperio,* meaning "open," supplied the name for ________________. The month ________________ got its name from Juno. Julius Caesar gave his name to ________________, and Augustus Caesar gave his name to ________________.

CAPITALIZING

Names of months

If you need help with capitalizing names of months, turn to Capitalization Rule 7 on page 119.

On the lines below, rewrite the paragraph given on the right. Capitalize the names of any months you find.

In january, Roy opened his own ice-cream store. He sold cherry ice cream in february and march. In april, he made turnip ice cream, but it didn't sell very well. He had more luck in may with bubblegum ice cream. So he sold it in june, too. The flavor of the month for july and august was watermelon. In september, he made apple ice cream. In october, lots of children came in for his pumpkin ice cream. Many people enjoyed his cranberry ice cream for dessert in november. His candy cane ice cream was a big hit for the holidays in december.

Writing Activity 1

If you need help, refer to the rules noted on pages 1–13.

Ever since you moved away from your hometown, you've missed seeing some of your relatives and friends. You all decide to have a reunion in a big hotel.

Fill in the blanks below. Be sure to capitalize correctly. You may make up information if you wish.

Your name (include your middle initial) ______________________________

What you call your parents and grandparents ______________________________

____

____

____

What you call two aunts and two uncles ______________________________

____

____

____

The names of three friends ______________________________

____

____

____

The names of three famous people (from books, movies, TV shows, or history) with whom you would like to spend time (include the people's titles)

____

____

____

The day of the week you arrived at the hotel ______________________________

The month, date, and year you arrived ______________________________

The day of the week you left the hotel ______________________________

The month, date, and year you left ______________________________

The story on the right describes your reunion. First fill in the blanks in the story, using the information you noted on page 14. Then finish the story on the lines below. Be sure to use *all* the information you listed on page 14.

I had looked forward for a long time to seeing the old gang. On ______________________________, my family and I arrived at the hotel. I used my full name, ______________________________, when I signed the register. After I found my room and unpacked, I went down to the dining room. There I saw lots of familiar faces. I saw my relatives and old friends. I even saw some famous people. Then the funniest thing happened. A waiter who was carrying a tray full of fancy food slipped on some butter. As he slid across the room, he grabbed at the tablecloths on the tables. Food and drinks splashed onto the guests. I was surprised at the different ways people reacted to the mess and confusion.

CAPITALIZING

Names of holidays

If you need help with capitalizing names of holidays, turn to Capitalization Rule 8 on page 119.

PRECHECK. In each sentence below, find the holiday name that should be capitalized. Then write the name correctly on the line next to the sentence. Check your answers at the bottom of the page.

1. Three presidents have died on the fourth of july. ______________________________
2. Abraham Lincoln made thanksgiving a national holiday. ______________________________
3. Memorial Day is also called decoration day. ______________________________
4. People make a lot of phone calls on mother's day. ______________________________
5. On april fools' day in 1898, the first car was sold. ______________________________

Number right: _____ *If less than 5, review the rule in the Reference Guide.*

The following paragraph is missing the names of holidays. Use the holidays listed on the left below to complete the paragraph. Be sure to capitalize the names of the holidays correctly.

discoverers' day
valentine's day
columbus day
halloween
new year's day
st. patrick's day

Jan and Frank were planning costume parties for the school year. For ______________________, people could dress as Father Time. For ______________________, people could be big red hearts. People could dress as elves or four-leaf clovers for ______________________. For ______________________, Jan and Frank didn't want everyone to dress up as Columbus. Then they remembered that in some places the day is called ______________________. So people could dress up as their favorite discoverers. For ______________________, Frank and Jan could just tell people to wear anything they wanted.

ANSWERS 1. Fourth of July 2. Thanksgiving 3. Decoration Day 4. Mother's Day 5. April Fools' Day

CAPITALIZING

Names of streets and highways
Names of cities and towns

If you need help with capitalizing names of streets, highways, cities, and towns, turn to Capitalization Rules 9 and 10 on page 119.

PRECHECK. In each sentence below, find the street, highway, city, or town name that should be capitalized. Then write the name correctly on the line next to the sentence. Check your answers at the bottom of the page.

1. Motown Records was founded in detroit. ______
2. The first paved street in the U.S. was stone street. ______
3. The first Super Bowl was held in los angeles. ______
4. The oldest subway system is in london. ______
5. Many of today's ads are created on madison avenue. ______

Number right: ____ *If less than 5, review the rules in the Reference Guide.*

CAPITALIZING

Names of streets and highways

Read the following sentences about Dan's search for a house to rent. In each sentence, find the street or highway name that should be capitalized. Then write the name correctly on the line next to the sentence.

1. Dan drove along route 66. ______
2. He took the lakeshore highway to the other side of town. ______
3. The house on bayview drive had a view of a garbage dump. ______
4. The place on shady lane was hot and dusty. ______
5. The house on pine street was right next to a lumber mill. ______
6. In the house on creekside avenue, the basement leaked. ______
7. Dan finally rented the white house on washington terrace. ______

ANSWERS 1. Detroit 2. Stone Street 3. Los Angeles 4. London 5. Madison Avenue

CAPITALIZING

Names of streets and highways

If you need help with capitalizing names of streets and highways, turn to Capitalization Rule 9 on page 119.

On the lines below, rewrite the paragraph given on the right. Capitalize the names of the streets and highways.

At twilight, Terry was driving down the bayshore highway. She decided to take a shortcut home. At the outer limits of the city, she took the parker boulevard exit. She went past the jail on newgate street. Then she saw the electric company on watt drive. She crossed states avenue and continued until she came to the parking lot at the corner of new york avenue and kentucky avenue. At ventnor avenue, she turned onto flushing way and drove past the water company. At short line street, she crossed some railroad tracks. She drove past the big red hotel on boardwalk terrace. Finally, she spotted her own little green house on mediterranean avenue.

CAPITALIZING

Names of cities and towns

If you need help with capitalizing names of cities and towns, turn to Capitalization Rule 10 on page 119.

In each sentence below, find the city or town name that should be capitalized. Then write the name correctly on the line next to the sentence.

1. Some people call boston "the hub of the universe." ______
2. "The biggest little city in the world" is reno. ______
3. The nickname for new york city is "the big apple." ______
4. "The city of light" refers to paris. ______
5. A common name for chicago is "the windy city." ______
6. "The garlic capital of the world" is gilroy. ______
7. People often call rome "the eternal city." ______
8. "The city of brotherly love" is philadelphia. ______

Rewrite the sentences below. Be sure to capitalize names of cities or towns.

1. The Mary Tyler Moore Show was set in minneapolis.

   ______

2. Li'l Abner lives in dogpatch.

   ______

3. The Dick Van Dyke Show took place in new rochelle.

   ______

4. Trapper John now works in a hospital in san francisco.

   ______

5. Laugh-In was broadcast from "beautiful downtown burbank."

   ______

CAPITALIZING

Names of cities and towns

If you need help with capitalizing names of cities and towns, turn to Capitalization Rule 10 on page 119.

On the lines below, rewrite the paragraph given on the right. Capitalize the names of cities or towns.

Robert was telling his friends about his exciting summer vacation. He enjoyed exploring the waterways near venice and rome. From there he went on to berlin and moscow. He spent a week in geneva. He liked cairo, but he found it too hot. He thought the gardens of amsterdam were beautiful. On his way home, he stopped in warsaw and dublin. His last week he spent close to home in toronto. And since all of these places are in Ohio, Robert did all this without ever leaving his home state!

CAPITALIZING

Names of cities and towns

If you need help with capitalizing names of cities and towns, turn to Capitalization Rule 10 on page 119.

The paragraph below this map is missing the names of the cities and towns. Use the map to help you fill in the blanks. Capitalize the names of the cities and towns correctly.

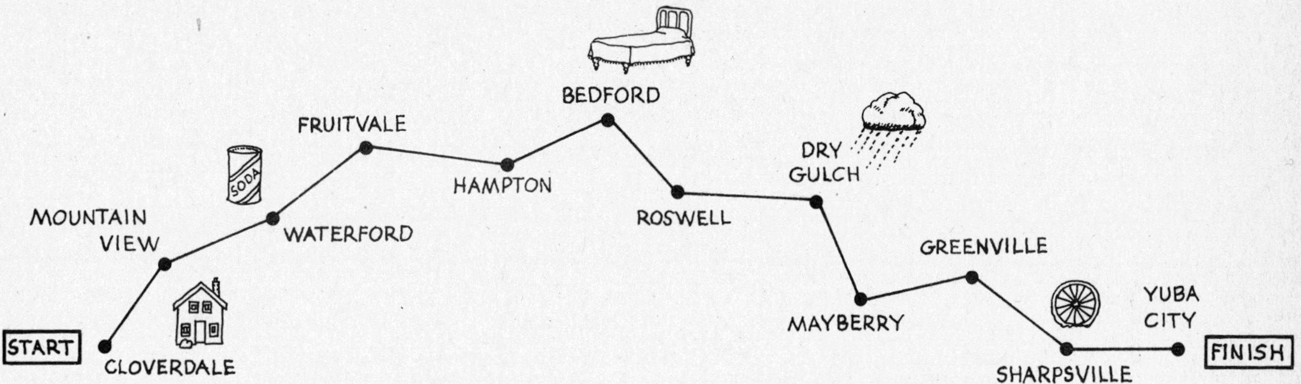

Mary and Fran took a bicycle trip. They started from their home in ______________________. They rested and admired the scenery in ______________________. Late in the morning, they stopped in ______________________ for a soda. They had lunch in ______________________ and dinner in ______________________. They spent the night at an inn in ______________________. The next day, they rode through ______________________. Later, they had to stop in ______________________ when it started raining. Then they went on to ______________________, where they spent the night with their cousin Andy. On the last day of the trip, they had a picnic lunch in ______________________. That afternoon, they stopped in ______________________, where Fran had to fix a flat tire. By evening, they reached their goal. They arrived in ______________________.

CAPITALIZING

Names of states, countries, and continents
Names of mountains and bodies of water

If you need help with capitalizing names of states, countries, continents, mountains, and bodies of water, turn to Capitalization Rules 11 and 12 on pages 119 and 120.

PRECHECK. In each sentence below, find the name of the state, country, continent, mountain, or body of water that should be capitalized. Then write the name correctly on the line next to the sentence. Check your answers at the bottom of the page.

1. A man climbed mount fuji in a wheelchair. ________________
2. The name for california came from a novel. ________________
3. Donald Duck was banned in finland for not wearing pants. ________________
4. Two men rowed across the atlantic ocean in 55 days. ________________
5. The first heart transplant was performed in africa. ________________

Number right: _____ *If less than 5, review the rules in the Reference Guide.*

CAPITALIZING

Names of states, countries, and continents

In each sentence below, find the name of the state, country, or continent that should be capitalized. Then write the name correctly on the line next to the sentence.

1. Bowling was invented in ancient egypt. ________________
2. In 1868, pennsylvania elected a dead man to Congress. ________________
3. The toothbrush was probably first used in china. ________________
4. The last queen of hawaii died in 1917. ________________
5. Playing cards appeared in europe in the 1300s. ________________
6. The clock was invented in asia in 725. ________________

ANSWERS 1. Mount Fuji 2. California 3. Finland 4. Atlantic Ocean 5. Africa

CAPITALIZING

Names of states, countries, and continents

If you need help with capitalizing names of states, countries, and continents, *turn to Capitalization Rule 11 on page 119.*

The paragraph below these travel ads is missing the names of states, countries, and continents. Use the travel ads to help you fill in the blanks. Capitalize the names of the states, countries, and continents correctly.

See **North America** *FIRST!*

Tour our northern neighbor, canada!
Watch the bullfights in mexico!
Spend a week in sunny florida!
See the movie stars of california!
Pan for gold in alaska!

DISCOVER EUROPE!

* * *

See the castles of ireland!
Climb the mountains of switzerland!
Visit the country inns of france!
Cruise down the rivers of germany!
See the windmills of holland!

Sam and Mark were looking at travel ads for the continents of ____________________ and ____________________. Sam wanted to take a leisurely cruise down the rivers of ____________________, but Mark wanted to lie on the beaches of sunny ____________________. Sam thought it would be fun to see the castles of ____________________. But Mark said he would rather see the movie stars of ____________________. Sam liked the idea of climbing the mountains of ____________________. Mark, however, hoped to get rich panning for gold in ____________________. Sam wanted to visit the country inns of ____________________ or the windmills of ____________________. But Mark said that if they wanted to leave the country, they should visit our northern neighbor, ____________________, or go to a bullfight in ____________________. They did agree on one thing—daydreams are cheaper than plane tickets.

CAPITALIZING

Names of mountains and bodies of water

If you need help with capitalizing names of mountains and bodies of water, turn to Capitalization Rule 12 on page 120.

In each sentence below, find the name of the mountain or body of water that should be capitalized. Then write the name correctly on the line next to the sentence.

1. Five blind boys climbed mount kenya in four days. ____________________
2. The oldest ocean is the pacific ocean. ____________________
3. Three hundred million ants live in the jura mountains. ____________________
4. The amazon river is named after ancient women warriors. ____________________
5. The world's largest freshwater lake is lake superior. ____________________

The paragraph on the right below is missing the names of mountains. Use the mountains in the list on the left below to complete the paragraph. Be sure to capitalize the names of the mountains correctly.

World's highest mountain:	mount everest
Highest mountain range:	himalayas
Highest unclimbed mountain:	zemu gap peak
World's lowest "official" hill:	bukit thompson
Highest mountain in Africa:	mount kilimanjaro

Mario and Phil wanted to go to the world's highest mountain range, the ____________________. They hoped to climb the world's highest mountain, ____________________, or the highest unclimbed mountain, ____________________. They also thought about going to Africa to climb ____________________ ____________________. But they decided first to climb the world's lowest hill, ____________________.

CAPITALIZING

Names of mountains and bodies of water

If you need help with capitalizing names of mountains and bodies of water, turn to Capitalization Rule 12 on page 120.

On the lines below, rewrite the paragraph given on the right. Capitalize the names of any bodies of water you find.

Strange things have been seen near many bodies of water. Many people have heard of the monster that lives in loch ness, a lake in Scotland. Other sea monsters are said to live in lake okanagan and lake simcoe in Canada. The green Creature from the Black Lagoon dwells in the amazon river. Some say a mermaid sits singing on a rock in the rhine river. Other mermaids have been seen in the arctic ocean. Sailors have also sighted a ghost ship in the atlantic ocean.

Writing Activity 2

If you need help, refer to the rules noted on pages 17–25.

Fill in the blanks below. Be sure to capitalize correctly.

The name of the continent you would most like to visit ______________________

The names of three states or countries you would like to visit on that continent ______________________

____

____

The names of three cities you would like to visit in those states or countries (you may make up the city names if you wish) ______________________

____

____

The names of a mountain, a river, and a lake you need to cross to get to the cities (you may make up the names if you wish) ______________________

____

____

On the lines below, write a paragraph describing a trip you might take to the places you have listed above. Be sure to use *all* of the names you have listed.

Fill in the blanks below. Be sure to capitalize correctly.

The name of a country you have made up ______________________________

The continent the country is on ______________________________

The two biggest states in the country ______________________________

____

The capital city of the country ______________________________

Two other major cities in the country ______________________________

____

The two tallest mountains in the country ______________________________

____

The two longest rivers in the country ______________________________

____

The two most beautiful lakes in the country ______________________________

____

The people of the country you have made up want more tourists to visit them. You have been asked to write a travel pamphlet. On the lines below, describe the wonderful sights tourists could see in this country. Be sure to use *all* of the information you listed above.

____

____

____

____

____

____

____

____

____

____

CAPITALIZING

Abbreviations

If you need help with capitalizing abbreviations, turn to Capitalization Rule 13 on page 120.

PRECHECK. In each sentence below, find the abbreviation that should be capitalized. Then write the abbreviation correctly on the line next to the sentence. Check your answers at the bottom of the page.

1. The most fumbles by a player in an nfl game is seven. ______
2. The longest speech given in the un took over four hours. ______
3. Clark Kent works at wgbs-tv. ______
4. There was once a feb. 30. ______
5. In the u.s.s.r., jeans sometimes sell for $140 a pair. ______

Number right: ____ *If less than 5, review the rule in the Reference Guide.*

In each sentence below, find the abbreviation that should be capitalized. Then write the abbreviation correctly on the line next to the sentence.

1. Nick works for the u.s. ______
2. He used to work for the fbi. ______
3. Now he is a spy for the cia. ______
4. He is working with nasa to protect our space secrets. ______
5. He also works with nato. ______
6. He reads secret documents from the u.s.s.r. ______
7. You will never see him on cbs. ______

ANSWERS 1. NFL 2. UN 3. WGBS-TV 4. Feb. 5. U.S.S.R.

CAPITALIZING

Abbreviations

If you need help with capitalizing abbreviations, turn to Capitalization Rule 13 on page 120.

The postal abbreviations for the states and the District of Columbia are given in this list. Some addresses are shown below the list. Rewrite the addresses on the blank lines. Use postal abbreviations in place of the state names.

Alabama—AL
Alaska—AK
Arizona—AZ
Arkansas—AR
California—CA
Colorado—CO
Connecticut—CT
Delaware—DE
Florida—FL
Georgia—GA
Hawaii—HI
Idaho—ID
Illinois—IL

Indiana—IN
Iowa—IA
Kansas—KS
Kentucky—KY
Louisiana—LA
Maine—ME
Maryland—MD
Massachusetts—MA
Michigan—MI
Minnesota—MN
Mississippi—MS
Missouri—MO
Montana—MT

Nebraska—NE
Nevada—NV
New Hampshire—NH
New Jersey—NJ
New Mexico—NM
New York—NY
North Carolina—NC
North Dakota—ND
Ohio—OH
Oklahoma—OK
Oregon—OR
Pennsylvania—PA
Rhode Island—RI

South Carolina—SC
South Dakota—SD
Tennessee—TN
Texas—TX
Utah—UT
Vermont—VT
Virginia—VA
Washington—WA
West Virginia—WV
Wisconsin—WI
Wyoming—WY
District of Columbia—DC

American Broadcasting Company
1330 Avenue of the Americas
New York, New York 10019

____
____
____

Grand Teton National Park
Drawer 170
Moose, Wyoming 83012

____
____
____

United Artists Records
6920 Sunset Boulevard
Los Angeles, California 90028

____
____
____

National Ding-a-Ling Club
P.O. Box 248
Melrose Park, Illinois 60160

____
____
____

CAPITALIZING

Abbreviations

If you need help with capitalizing abbreviations, turn to Capitalization Rule 13 on page 120.

On the lines below, rewrite the paragraph given on the right. Capitalize any abbreviations you find. (Do not spell out the abbreviated words.)

On wed., April 18, 1906, San Francisco was shaken by an earthquake. It happened at 5:13 in the morning. Leaking gas lines and overturned stoves started fires south of Market st. Soon there was a huge fire where Third st. and Mission st. join. Both the Spreckels bldg. and the Hearst bldg., where the s.f. newspapers were published, burned down. To stop the spread of the fire, fire fighters dynamited buildings east of Van Ness ave. The fire was put out on sat., April 21. On fri., April 27, the u.s. Army was ordered to help rebuild the city and keep order.

CAPITALIZING

Titles of works

If you need help with capitalizing titles of works, turn to Capitalization Rule 14 on page 120.

PRECHECK. In each sentence below, find the title that should be capitalized. Then write the title correctly on the line next to the sentence. Check your answers at the bottom of the page.

1. Abraham Lincoln wrote "the trailor murder mystery." ________________
2. The book dune was rejected by 13 publishers. ________________
3. The world's most popular song is "happy birthday to you." ________________
4. The family in leave it to beaver is named Cleaver. ________________
5. Bette Davis starred in jezebel. ________________

Number right: _____ *If less than 5, review the rule in the Reference Guide.*

In each sentence below, find the title that should be capitalized. Then write the title correctly on the line next to the sentence.

1. James Bond's first movie was casino royale. ________________
2. The author of how the world began was four years old. ________________
3. The solo album thriller set a sales record. ________________
4. A nineteenth-century newspaper was called the bazoo. ________________
5. A play called the exile is only three sentences long. ________________
6. The car in my mother the car was a 1928 Porter. ________________
7. The writer of the Southern song "dixie" was a Northerner. ________________

ANSWERS 1. "The Trailor Murder Mystery" 2. Dune 3. "Happy Birthday to You" 4. Leave It to Beaver 5. Jezebel

CAPITALIZING

Titles of works

If you need help with capitalizing titles of works, turn to Capitalization Rule 14 on page 120.

Rewrite the song titles below. Be sure to capitalize the titles correctly.

1. "i scream, you scream, we all scream for ice cream"

2. "plant a watermelon on my grave, and let the juice soak through"

3. "where did robinson crusoe go with friday on saturday night?"

4. "come after breakfast, bring your lunch, and leave before suppertime"

5. "how could you believe me when i said i love you when you know i've been a liar all my life?"

6. "i've got those wake up seven-thirty, wash your ears, they're dirty, eat your eggs and oatmeal, rush to school blues"

CAPITALIZING

Titles of works

If you need help with capitalizing titles of works, turn to Capitalization Rule 14 on page 120.

On the lines below, rewrite the paragraph given on the right. Capitalize the titles of any movies or television shows you find.

Many famous actors have appeared in horror films. Before James Arness starred in gunsmoke, he was in the thing. Humphrey Bogart appeared in the return of dr. x. Charles Bronson was in house of wax, and Donald Sutherland was in castle of the living dead. When teenage horror films were popular, Robert Vaughn starred in teenage caveman. In the blob, Steve McQueen also played a teenager. Michael Landon is now known for bonanza, little house on the prairie, and highway to heaven. But his first film was i was a teenage werewolf.

CAPITALIZING

Proper nouns
Proper adjectives

If you need help with capitalizing proper nouns and proper adjectives, turn to Capitalization Rules 15 and 16 on page 120.

PRECHECK. In each sentence below, find the proper noun or proper adjective that should be capitalized. Then write the word or term correctly on the line next to the sentence. Check your answers at the bottom of the page.

1. The first medal of honor was awarded in 1863. ______
2. Moscow is the home of the bolshoi ballet. ______
3. Nazis once forced a german author to eat his own book. ______
4. Richard Nixon played football for whittier college. ______
5. The british people use the most soap. ______

Number right: ____ *If less than 5, review the rules in the Reference Guide.*

CAPITALIZING

Proper nouns

In each sentence below, find the proper noun that should be capitalized. Then write the noun correctly on the line next to the sentence.

1. The treaty of versailles ended World War I. ______
2. Ronald Reagan was once a member of the democratic party. ______
3. In 1927, the first academy awards were given. ______
4. Ancient egyptians considered cats sacred. ______
5. We stayed at the hyatt hotel in New York. ______
6. There are picketers camped outside the white house. ______
7. The magna carta was signed in 1215. ______

ANSWERS 1. Medal of Honor 2. Bolshoi Ballet 3. German 4. Whittier College 5. British

CAPITALIZING

Proper nouns

If you need help with capitalizing proper nouns, turn to Capitalization Rule 15 on page 120.

On the lines below, rewrite the paragraph given on the right. Capitalize any proper nouns you find.

There are many wonders of the world. One is the great pyramid in Egypt. Other wonders include the hanging gardens of babylon and a huge statue, the colossus of rhodes. Some other wonders of the world are the colosseum in Rome and the great wall of china. The famous leaning tower of pisa and stonehenge are also wonders. Some modern wonders are the empire state building, the golden gate bridge, and hoover dam.

CAPITALIZING

Proper adjectives

If you need help with capitalizing proper adjectives, turn to Capitalization Rule 16 on page 120.

In each sentence below, find the proper adjective that should be capitalized. Then write the adjective correctly on the line next to the sentence.

1. The most popular american food is fried chicken. ______
2. I have michelin tires on my new car. ______
3. The hamburger probably is asian in origin. ______
4. Butter was used as a greek hairdressing. ______
5. My grandmother used only granny smith apples in pies. ______
6. The swedish people drink the most coffee. ______
7. The arbor day holiday began in Nebraska. ______

Rewrite the sentences below. Make sure you capitalize each proper adjective.

1. The chinese people once used tea for money.

   ______

2. The roman poet Virgil gave a funeral for a fly.

   ______

3. <u>As You Like It</u> is a shakespearean play.

   ______

4. You can't run if you cut your achilles tendon.

   ______

5. Tarzan was an english nobleman.

   ______

CAPITALIZING

Direct quotations

If you need help with capitalizing direct quotations, turn to Capitalization Rule 17 on page 120.

PRECHECK. In each sentence below, find the word that should be capitalized. Then write the word correctly on the line next to the sentence. Check your answers at the bottom of the page.

1. Franklin said, "fish and visitors stink in three days." __________
2. Mark Twain asked, "is the human race a joke?" __________
3. Emerson claimed, "politeness ruins conversations." __________
4. The proverb says, "a fool and his money are soon parted." __________
5. Queen Victoria said, "we are not amused." __________

Number right: _____ *If less than 5, review the rule in the Reference Guide.*

In each sentence below, find the word that should be capitalized. Then write the word correctly on the line next to the sentence.

1. Captain Marvel often says, "holy moley!" __________
2. Alfred E. Neuman asks, "what? Me worry?" __________
3. Maxwell Smart says, "sorry about that, Chief." __________
4. The cast of Laugh-In says, "sock it to me!" __________
5. Those cartoon shows end, "that's all, folks!" __________
6. Bugs Bunny asks, "what's up, Doc?" __________
7. The Lone Ranger cries, "hi-yo, Silver! Away!" __________

ANSWERS 1. Fish 2. Is 3. Politeness 4. A 5. We

CAPITALIZING

Direct quotations

If you need help with capitalizing direct quotations, turn to Capitalization Rule 17 on page 120.

On the lines below, rewrite the paragraph given on the right. Capitalize the first word of any direct quotations you find.

Many famous people wrote words for their grave markers. W. C. Fields wrote, "on the whole, I'd rather be in Philadelphia." G. B. Shaw suggested, "i knew if I stayed around long enough, something like this would happen." Hemingway wanted written, "pardon me for not getting up." Robert Benchley wrote, "this is all over my head." Fredric March proposed, "this is just my lot." William Haines suggested, "here's something I want to get off my chest." Probably none of these sayings were really used.

CAPITALIZING

Greetings and closings in letters

If you need help with capitalizing greetings and closings in letters, turn to Capitalization Rule 18 on page 120.

The greetings for some letters are given below. Rewrite them on the lines that follow. Make sure you capitalize the greetings correctly.

dear Mom,

____

dear Sir or Madam:

____

dear Senator Cranston:

____

dear Auntie Mame,

____

my dear Miss Post:

____

dear Mr. Spock:

____

dear Jim,

____

dear Colonel Klink:

____

Some closings for letters are given below. Rewrite them on the lines that follow. Make sure you capitalize the closings correctly.

love,
Jeff

____

____

best wishes,
Mary

____

____

sincerely yours,
Linda Chan

____

____

yours very truly,
Steven B. Simpson

____

____

fondly,
Jane

____

____

affectionately,
Bill

____

____

CAPITALIZING

Outlines

If you need help with capitalizing outlines, turn to Capitalization Rule 19 on page 120.

On the lines below, rewrite the outline given on the right. Be sure to capitalize correctly and to put periods after the outline letters and numbers.

Horror Movies

i main types
    a monsters and vampires
    b ghosts and aliens
ii settings
    a graveyards
    b castles and dungeons
    c science labs
iii special effects

CAPITALIZING

Outlines

If you need help with capitalizing outlines, turn to Capitalization Rule 19 on page 120.

One section of an outline is detailed on the right. Rewrite the section on the lines below. Be sure to capitalize correctly and to put periods after the outline letters and numbers.

iii special effects
- a makeup
  - 1 blood and gore
    - a black-and-white movies
    - b color movies
  - 2 aging
  - 3 creatures
- b sound effects
- c lighting effects
- d stunts

Writing Activity 3

If you need help, refer to the rules noted on pages 40 and 41.

Read the paragraph given on the right. Then fill in all the blanks in the outline at the bottom of the page. Don't forget to capitalize the outline letters and numbers as well as words, where necessary.

Have you ever spent the whole day watching TV? If you're in the mood to be educated, you can watch educational shows. Some, such as Sesame Street and The Electric Company, are for children. Others, such as Sunrise Semester and Voice of Agriculture, are for adults. Then maybe you'll want to play along with the game shows. Or perhaps you'd rather watch old movies instead. You can almost always find a war movie or a western. If you want something shorter, you can watch a rerun of an old TV show. You can choose a comedy such as M*A*S*H or I Love Lucy. Or you can watch something more adventurous, such as Star Trek or Mission: Impossible.

DAYTIME TV SHOWS

I. Educational TV shows

A. Shows for children

______

2. ______

B. Shows for adults

______

______

II. Game shows

III. ______

______

B. Westerns

IV. Reruns of old TV shows

______

1. M*A*S*H

______

B. Adventure shows

______

______

PUNCTUATING

Punctuation marks at the ends of sentences

If you need help with end punctuation, turn to Punctuation Rule 1 on page 121.

PRECHECK. On the line next to each sentence below, write the correct end punctuation mark. Check your answers at the bottom of the page.

1. Israel has issued identity cards to its cattle__________
2. Did you know that there is an IQ test for dogs__________
3. A beheaded cockroach can live up to seven days__________
4. How does a giraffe sit down__________
5. Ants milk aphids the way we milk cows__________

Number right: _____ *If less than 5, review the rule in the Reference Guide.*

On the line next to each sentence below, write the correct end punctuation mark.

1. What could Thomas Adams make from tree sap__________
2. Maybe he could make rubber or a false-teeth adhesive__________
3. In the end, all he could make was chewing gum__________
4. Big deal__________
5. More than 50 years later, bubblegum was invented__________
6. Do you know why most bubblegum is pink__________
7. Pink was the only color of dye that bubblegum's inventor had__________

ANSWERS 1. period (.) 2. question mark (?) 3. exclamation point (!) or period (.) 4. question mark (?) 5. period (.)

PUNCTUATING

Punctuation marks at the ends of sentences

If you need help with end punctuation, turn to Punctuation Rule 1 on page 121.

On the lines below, rewrite the paragraph given on the right. Be sure to end each sentence with the correct punctuation mark.

Have you ever heard the story of Jonah   He was supposedly swallowed by a whale   In 1891, an English sailor had the same experience   His whaling ship captured a whale   The whale overturned his boat   The sailor was swallowed by the whale   After his shipmates killed the whale, they saw its stomach move   They cut open the stomach and found the missing sailor   What a surprise The sailor was unconscious, but he was still alive   What does it feel like to be swallowed by a whale   The sailor said that the whale's insides were slippery   It was also very hot inside   The sailor's skin was bleached white by the whale's stomach juices   It stayed that way for the rest of his life

PUNCTUATING

Periods with abbreviations
Periods after initials

If you need help with periods with abbreviations and after initials, turn to Punctuation Rules 2 and 3 on page 121.

PRECHECK. On the line next to each sentence below, write the abbreviation or initials you find in the sentence. Be sure to punctuate correctly. Check your answers at the bottom of the page.

1. A student told his teacher his name was Art E Choke. __________
2. A woman let her hair grow to be 10½ ft long. __________
3. One of James Bond's archenemies is Dr No. __________
4. Someone named a child I O Silver. __________
5. A talking horse named Mr Ed once had his own show. __________

Number right: _____ *If less than 5, review the rules in the Reference Guide.*

PUNCTUATING

Periods with abbreviations

On the line next to each sentence below, write the abbreviation you find in the sentence. Be sure to punctuate correctly.

1. Mrs O'Leary's cow supposedly started the Chicago Fire. __________
2. Capt America's real name is Steve Rogers. __________
3. Margaret Houlihan, R N, is also known as Hotlips. __________
4. The house at 221B Baker St was Sherlock Holmes's. __________
5. The last baseball triple-header was on Oct 2, 1920. __________
6. Abraham Lincoln was shot at 10:30 P M on April 14, 1865. __________
7. Egg City, near L A, contains two million chickens. __________

ANSWERS 1. E. 2. ft. 3. Dr. 4. I. O. 5. Mr.

PUNCTUATING

Periods with abbreviations

If you need help with periods with abbreviations, turn to Punctuation Rule 2 on page 121.

On the lines below, rewrite the paragraph given on the right. Be sure to punctuate the abbreviations correctly.

There have been pancake races in England since 1445 A D. Each runner tosses a pancake in a pan three times along a course 415 yd long. The record time of 61.0 sec was set by Ms Sally Ann Faulkner on Feb 26, 1974. The U S record of 58.5 sec was set in 1975. Mr Dale Lyons tosses a pancake while he runs marathons. He tosses a 2-oz pancake in a 1½-lb pan. On Mar 25, 1984, he ran a pancake marathon in 2 hr 57 min 16 sec.

PUNCTUATING

Periods after initials

If you need help with periods after initials, turn to Punctuation Rule 3 on page 121.

In each sentence below, find a person's name. Then write the name on the line next to the sentence. Be sure to punctuate the initials correctly.

1. Former president Gerald R Ford was once a model. ________________
2. Inventor Thomas A Edison began a science fiction novel. ________________
3. Mrs. E Hodges was hit by a meteorite. ________________
4. G Pennypacker became a general when he was only 20. ________________
5. A P Giannini classified his Rolls Royce as a fire engine. ________________
6. The doughnut hole was invented by H C Gregory. ________________
7. L Weiser owns a car over 26 feet long. ________________

Rewrite each sentence below. Be sure to punctuate the initials correctly.

1. J Fred Muggs was the chimpanzee on <u>The Today Show</u>.

   ____

2. Yuri A Gagarin was the first man in space.

   ____

3. The parking meter was invented by Carl C Magee.

   ____

4. Erle Stanley Gardner also used the name of A A Fair.

   ____

5. Esther P Friedman is better known as Ann Landers.

   ____

PUNCTUATING

Periods after initials

If you need help with periods after initials, turn to Punctuation Rule 3 on page 121.

The paragraph given on the right is missing the initials of the people mentioned. Rewrite the paragraph on the lines below, supplying the missing initials. Be sure to punctuate the initials correctly.

Many people are known by their initials rather than their full names. The comedian William Claude Fields is better known as ___ Fields. The circus showman Phineas Taylor Barnum is more famous as ___ Barnum. We think of Benjamin Franklin Goodrich as ___ Goodrich, and we know James Cash Penney as ___ Penney. Sometimes people think that ___ Simpson's initials stand for orange juice, but they really stand for Orenthal James. The actor ___ Marshall says that his initials mean "Everybody's Guess."

PUNCTUATING

Commas in dates
Commas in place names

If you need help with commas in dates and in place names, turn to Punctuation Rules 4 and 5 on page 121.

PRECHECK. On the line next to each sentence below, write the date or place name you find in the sentence. Be sure to punctuate the date or name correctly. Check your answers at the bottom of the page.

1. In Toledo Spain, it's illegal to walk more than two abreast. ______
2. The first drive-in movie opened on June 6 1933. ______
3. On March 2 1962 Wilt Chamberlain scored 100 points. ______
4. The first U.S. newspaper ad was published on May 1 1704. ______
5. No witch was ever burned in Salem Massachusetts. ______

Number right: ______ *If less than 5, review the rules in the Reference Guide.*

PUNCTUATING

Commas in dates

On the line next to each sentence below, write the date you find in the sentence. Be sure to punctuate the date correctly.

1. August 18 1902 saw the first unassisted triple play. ______
2. Direct-dial long-distance calls began on October 10 1951. ______
3. The first adhesive postage stamp appeared on May 1 1840. ______
4. On February 10 1933 the first singing telegram was sent. ______
5. Men first rode in a balloon on October 15 1783. ______
6. On April 2 1877 the first human cannonball was fired. ______
7. July 20 1969 was the day men first landed on the moon. ______

ANSWERS 1. Toledo, Spain 2. June 6, 1933 3. March 2, 1962, 4. May 1, 1704 5. Salem, Massachusetts

PUNCTUATING

Commas in dates

If you need help with commas in dates, turn to Punctuation Rule 4 on page 121.

On the lines below, rewrite the paragraph given on the right. Be sure to punctuate the dates correctly.

Jake and Sandy finished their time machine on October 30 3149. They set the dial to July 1 1972 and attended the World Championship Watermelon Seed-Spitting Contest. Then they traveled to February 1 1970 and saw a swamp-buggy race. August 11 1972 found them at the Annual Hobo Convention. They watched a man eat a birch tree on September 11 1980. On May 6 1972 they went to a turtle race, and on September 13 1969 they attended Swap, Talk, and Brag Day. They watched the World Clam-Gulping Championship on April 18 1970. They returned home on November 6 3149 and told everybody what they had found out about the eating habits and social lives of prehistoric people.

PUNCTUATING

Commas in place names

If you need help with commas in place names, turn to Punctuation Rule 5 on page 121.

On the line next to each sentence below, write the complete place name you find in the sentence. Be sure to punctuate the name correctly.

1. The first Ferris wheel opened in Chicago Illinois. ______
2. A man in Santa Clara California has 1,159 credit cards. ______
3. The world's oldest zoo is in Vienna Austria. ______
4. The first gas station opened in Bordeaux France. ______
5. In Enterprise Alabama stands a statue of a boll weevil. ______
6. A female boxer beat a male opponent in Mexico City Mexico. ______
7. Basketball was invented in Springfield Massachusetts. ______

Rewrite the sentences below. Be sure to punctuate the place names correctly.

1. The All-American Soap Box Derby is in Akron Ohio.

   ______

2. A horsemeat banquet was held in London England in 1868.

   ______

3. The Gateway Arch is located in St. Louis Missouri.

   ______

4. The Dodgers were once a Brooklyn New York team.

   ______

5. In Moscow U.S.S.R. a circus has cows that play football.

   ______

PUNCTUATING

Commas in place names

If you need help with commas in place names, turn to Punctuation Rule 5 on page 121.

The following paragraph is missing the names of cities and states. Use the place names listed on the left below to help you complete the paragraph. Be sure to punctuate the place names correctly.

Athens Tennessee
Vienna Missouri
Geneva New York
Timbuctoo California
Cuba Missouri
Geneva Nebraska
Athens Georgia
Moscow Idaho
Paris Texas
Waterloo Iowa

Rita and Greg hoped to become world travelers someday. They wanted to see the ruins of Athens, Greece, but their budget would carry them only as far as ________________ or ________________. They would need to brush up on their Spanish if they went to Cuba, but not if they went to ________________. If they went to Geneva, Switzerland, they could see the Alps. But they weren't sure if there were any mountains in ________________ or ________________. They could visit the music halls of Vienna, Austria, or go to a rock concert in ________________. Travel to ________________ would probably be easier than to Moscow, U.S.S.R. Somehow they thought Paris, France, would be more exciting than ________________. They wanted to see the battlefield of Waterloo, Belgium, but knew that they might have to settle for ________________. They were most excited about going to the famous African town of Timbuktu, Mali. They just hoped they wouldn't end up in its namesake, the ghost town of ________________.

PUNCTUATING

Commas in place names

If you need help with commas in place names, turn to Punctuation Rule 5 on page 121.

On the lines below, rewrite the paragraph given on the right. Be sure to punctuate the place names correctly.

The names of many American cities and towns are unusual. For instance, there are a Cotton Plant Arkansas and a Yazoo City Mississippi. Perhaps Fiddletown California has more than its share of fiddlers. But does Thief River Falls Minnesota have more than its share of thieves? You might wonder how Crowheart Wyoming got its name, or whether Dinosaur Colorado is about to become extinct. In Bad Axe Michigan would you expect to have your axe fixed or have it broken? And in Wartburg Tennessee would you expect to get warts or to have them cured?

Writing Activity 4

If you need help, refer to the rules noted on pages 45–53.

The Voter Registration Form given on the right has been filled in to remind you of some of the rules you have learned. Fill out the form below, using your own name and personal data. Use as many abbreviations as possible.

Voter Registration Form

Name: Rocky (First Name) C. (Middle Initial) Beach (Last Name)

Address: 257 Lakeshore Ave. (Number and Street) Apt. 17 (Apartment Number)

Surf, (City) CA (State) 94530 (ZIP Code)

Date of Birth: Aug. (Month) 14, (Day) 1961 (Year)

Birthplace: Riverton, (City) MA (State (Country if not U.S.))

Political Party: WHIG

Signature: Rocky C. Beach

Voter Registration Form

Name: ______________________________

First Name Middle Initial Last Name

Address: ______________________________

Number and Street Apartment Number

____

City State ZIP Code

Date of Birth: ______________________________

Month Day Year

Birthplace: ______________________________

City State (Country if not U.S.)

Political Party: ______________________________

Signature: ______________________________

Fill out the following Job Application. You may make up information if you wish. Use as many abbreviations as possible.

Job Application

Today's date: ______________________________

Name: ____
First Name Middle Initial Last Name

Address: ____
Number and Street Apartment Number

____
City State ZIP Code

Date of birth: ____
Month Day Year

Place of birth: ____
City State Country

On what date can you start work? ______________________________
Month Day Year

Current occupation: ______________________________

Name and address of current employer
(If you are a student, give the name and address of your school.)

____
Name

____
Number and Street

____
City State ZIP Code

Name and address of someone who can recommend you:

____
First Name Middle Initial Last Name

____
Number and Street Apartment Number

____
City State ZIP Code

PUNCTUATING

Commas in compound sentences

If you need help with commas in compound sentences, turn to Punctuation Rule 6 on page 122.

PRECHECK. Each of the following sentences is missing a comma. In each sentence, put in the comma. Then, on the line next to the sentence, write the word that comes before the comma, the comma itself, and the word that follows the comma. Check your answers at the bottom of the page.

1. Insects outnumber us and they also outweigh us. ____________
2. Barbers now cut hair but they once also did surgery. ____________
3. Paper contains an acid and the acid destroys the paper in 50 years. ____________
4. A ballpoint pen can write on paper or it can write on butter. ____________
5. Cats are very small but they have more bones than we do. ____________

Number right: ____ *If less than 5, review the rule in the Reference Guide.*

Rewrite the sentences below. Be sure to put commas before the coordinating conjunctions.

1. The ostrich cannot fly and the penguin cannot fly, either.

   ____

2. Spencer Tracy won an Oscar but it said, "To Dick Tracy."

   ____

3. Sugarless gum has six calories and regular gum has eight.

   ____

4. Bathtubs can be used for bathing or they can be used for racing.

   ____

ANSWERS 1. us, and 2. hair, but 3. acid, and 4. paper, or 5. small, but

PUNCTUATING

Commas in compound sentences

If you need help with commas in compound sentences, turn to Punctuation Rule 6 on page 122.

On the lines below, rewrite the paragraph given on the right. Be sure to punctuate the compound sentences correctly.

You can go to an auction and you can see people bidding in the strangest ways. People sometimes shout their bids but that can make an auction very noisy. Instead, buyers often wiggle their noses to make a bid or they tug at their ears. Some bidders shrug their shoulders and others tip their hats. People may need to scratch their noses when they itch but they may not want to buy anything. Some people are afraid of making an accidental bid and they don't move at all. These people worry a lot but a good auctioneer can tell when a bid is really being made. Bidders tell the auctioneer their signals ahead of time and the auctioneer knows what to look for. At an auction, you can wiggle your nose all you want and you don't have to worry about buying an ugly antique you can't afford.

PUNCTUATING

Commas in compound sentences

If you need help with commas in compound sentences, turn to Punctuation Rule 6 on page 122.

Some pairs of sentences are given below. Use one of the coordinating conjunctions listed on the left below to combine each pair of sentences. Write the new sentences on the lines provided. Don't forget to put a comma before the coordinating conjunction.

and
but
or

1. Cold drinks seem to cool you down.
   Hot drinks really cool you down.

   ____

   ____

2. Doggydent toothpaste for dogs tastes like beef.
   It sells for five dollars a tube.

   ____

   ____

3. Thomas Paine was an American statesman.
   He first worked as a corset maker.

   ____

   ____

4. Clarence Darrow was a successful lawyer.
   He never graduated from law school.

   ____

   ____

5. To get rich, you can work very hard.
   You can have rich parents.

   ____

   ____

PUNCTUATING

Commas in compound sentences

If you need help with commas in compound sentences, turn to Punctuation Rule 6 on page 122.

The following paragraph is missing some conjunctions. Use the coordinating conjunctions listed on the left below to complete the paragraph. Be sure to put a comma before each coordinating conjunction.

and
but
or

Randy and Lisa didn't have much free time __________ they wanted to go to a movie. They turned to the movie section in the newspaper __________ they looked through the listings. They could go see an adventure film __________ they could go see a comedy. Randy liked suspense movies __________ he suggested the latest James Bond movie. Lisa liked suspense movies, too __________ she felt like seeing something funny. There was a Richard Pryor movie downtown __________ there was a Steve Martin movie in the neighborhood. Randy had just seen the Steve Martin movie __________ they decided against that. He wanted to see the Richard Pryor movie __________ they didn't have time to go all the way downtown. Time was running out __________ they had to decide soon. They had to reach a compromise __________ they wouldn't have time to see anything. Then they saw a listing for the perfect movie. It clearly had lots of suspense __________ it also sounded very funny. They got their coats __________ they went to see The Attack of the Killer Tomatoes.

PUNCTUATING

Commas in series

If you need help with commas in series, turn to Punctuation Rule 7 on page 122.

PRECHECK. **On the line below each sentence, write the series found in the sentence. Be sure to include commas. Check your answers at the bottom of the page.**

1. One bus company will not allow its passengers to carry corpses live snakes or fuel tanks.

   ____

2. Early to bed and early to rise makes a man healthy wealthy and boring.

   ____

3. He caught the fish cleaned it broiled it and went out for pizza.

   ____

4. A skull 180,000 dead cats and Judy Garland's false eyelashes have all been sold at auctions.

   ____

Number right: _____ *If less than 4, review the rule in the Reference Guide.*

Rewrite each sentence below. Be sure to punctuate the series correctly.

1. Various cultures throw rice wheat or raw eggs at brides.

   ____

2. She went over a river through a woods and up a creek.

   ____

3. Monkeys are clever quick deceitful and almost human.

   ____

4. The French are famous for wine perfume and fries.

   ____

ANSWERS 1. corpses, live snakes, or fuel tanks 2. healthy, wealthy, and boring 3. caught the fish, cleaned it, broiled it, and went out for pizza 4. A skull, 180,000 dead cats, and Judy Garland's false eyelashes

PUNCTUATING

Commas in series

If you need help with commas in series, turn to Punctuation Rule 7 on page 122.

Use the list on the left below to help you complete the following paragraph. In each blank, fill in a series of at least three items from the list. Use as many of the items as you can. You may use an item more than once. Don't forget that each series needs commas and either "and" or "or."

mashed potatoes
spaghetti
French fries
chocolate chips
peanut butter
chocolate milk
enchiladas
apple pie
hot fudge
peas
pancakes
pepper
onion rings
bologna
ice cream
gravy
chow mein
brownies
orange juice
raisins
pickles
cookies
syrup
sugar
tomatoes
soda
hot dogs
pizza
onions
cereal
cheese
coffee
ketchup
iced tea

Some of my friends have the strangest eating habits. For instance, Jeff eats ______________________________ ______ for breakfast. To wash it all down, he drinks ______ ______________________________. And he's not as bad as Anna, who puts ______________________ ______________ on her eggs. For lunch, Brad often makes a sandwich that has ______________________ ______________ in it. For dessert, he has ______ ______________________________. Like many people, Tina has popcorn at the movies, but she sprinkles ______ ______________________________ on it. It's hard to tell what meal Stan is eating in the evening because he has ______________________________ with ______________________________ ______. Over it all he pours ______________________ ______________. For a midnight snack, Felipe has ______________________________ ______. I don't know how he can sleep after that, but he is always hungry for a breakfast of ______________________ ______________.

PUNCTUATING

Commas in series

If you need help with commas in series, turn to Punctuation Rule 7 on page 122.

On the lines below, rewrite the paragraph given on the right. Be sure to punctuate the series correctly.

There are many ways to clean a chimney. Today, people use shovels rods brushes and flashlights. In the 1800s, people brushed the chimney with evergreens rattled chains against the chimney walls or sent boys up the chimney. The boys were poor small and helpless. Their work was dirty dangerous and difficult. They could be hurt by falling bricks burnt by hot ashes or choked by soot. They were badly paid badly fed and badly treated. The boys' master, the chimney sweep, had an easier life. People thought he brought luck, so they wanted to touch his brushes shake his hand or kiss him.

PUNCTUATING

Commas after introductory phrases and clauses

If you need help with commas after introductory phrases and clauses, turn to Punctuation Rule 8 on page 122.

PRECHECK. Each of the following sentences is missing a comma. In each sentence, put in the comma. Then, on the line next to the sentence, write the word that comes before the comma, the comma itself, and the word that follows the comma. Check your answers at the bottom of the page.

1. Although they look peaceful butterflies are warlike. ____________________
2. In 1934 men were fined for wearing topless bathing suits. ____________________
3. After 19 years on the air <u>Gunsmoke</u> was cancelled. ____________________
4. Because he was big President Taft used a special bathtub. ____________________
5. Across the Snake River there is a bridge made of junk. ____________________

Number right: _____ *If less than 5, review the rule in the Reference Guide.*

Rewrite the sentences below. Be sure to put commas after the introductory phrases and clauses.

1. In a garden in England a man lived 20 years in a box.

   ____

2. Compared to dogs and cats pigs are very smart.

   ____

3. After stealing 15,000 books a man said, "I like to read."

   ____

4. Although it seems American the log cabin is Swedish.

   ____

5. When they lie down people grow taller.

   ____

ANSWERS 1. peaceful, butterflies 2. 1934, men 3. air, <u>Gunsmoke</u> 4. big, President 5. River, there

PUNCTUATING

Commas after introductory phrases and clauses

If you need help with commas after introductory phrases and clauses, turn to Punctuation Rule 8 on page 122.

The paragraph below this list is missing introductory phrases and clauses. Use the items in the list to complete the paragraph. The first item on the list goes in the first blank, the second item in the second blank, and so forth. Be sure to put a comma after each introductory phrase or clause.

Last Saturday
After I fought with my sister
To calm down
When my mother yelled at me
Since she was yelling
By then
While I was combing my hair
With everything going wrong
As I turned the corner
As a result
Once I was at work
If I were going to get yelled at
By the time I got home

____________________ I really had a bad day. ____________________ I just wanted to be left alone. ____________________ I turned on the stereo. ____________________ I turned it off. ____________________ I couldn't hear the music anyway. ____________________ it was time to go to work. ____________________ the comb broke. ____________________ I knew I would be late. ____________________ the bus pulled away. ____________________ I had to walk. ____________________ my boss yelled at me for listening to the radio. ____________________ I might just as well have stayed home. ____________________ everybody else had already eaten, including the dog. My hamburger was gone.

PUNCTUATING

Commas after introductory phrases and clauses

If you need help with commas after introductory phrases and clauses, turn to Punctuation Rule 8 on page 122.

Rewrite the sentences below. Be sure to put commas after the introductory phrases and clauses.

1. Once in a while a whole group of people imagines the same thing.

2. About 30 years ago one of the most famous cases occurred.

3. In a hospital in London 300 doctors and nurses thought they had polio.

4. Because there were no polio shots then people were very afraid of polio.

5. Although the doctors and nurses seemed to have the disease tests showed they did not.

6. After a short time everybody got better.

7. To everyone's surprise it was mostly the doctors and nurses who imagined that they had polio.

8. Although they were already sick few of the patients believed they had polio.

PUNCTUATING

Commas after introductory phrases and clauses

If you need help with commas after introductory phrases and clauses, turn to Punctuation Rule 8 on page 122.

On the lines below, rewrite the paragraph given on the right. Be sure to put commas after introductory phrases and clauses.

In San Jose, California there is a house known as the Winchester Mystery House. After Sarah Winchester's husband died she inherited his fortune. Because the fortune came from the sales of the popular Winchester rifle she felt guilty. Afraid of being haunted by the ghosts of people killed with the rifle she built a house to protect herself. To fool the spirits who might be after her she built rooms with no doors. High up the walls of beautiful rooms windows look only into other rooms. At the top of grand staircases doors open onto walls. Because she believed that she would stay alive as long as the house was unfinished Mrs. Winchester kept adding on to it. When she died the house had 160 rooms, 200 doors, 10,000 windowpanes, and 47 fireplaces.

PUNCTUATING

Commas with nouns of address

If you need help using commas with nouns of address, turn to Punctuation Rule 9 on page 122.

PRECHECK. In each sentence below, find the noun of address. Then write it on the line next to the sentence. Be sure to include the comma or commas that belong with it. Check your answers at the bottom of the page.

1. Popeye eat your carrots! ______________________
2. Where is the Temple of Doom Indiana Jones? ______________________
3. I'm suing you Dr. Welby for malpractice. ______________________
4. Members of the jury what is your verdict? ______________________
5. For once Perry Mason your client is guilty. ______________________

Number right: ______ *If less than 5, review the rule in the Reference Guide.*

Rewrite the sentences below. Be sure to punctuate the nouns of address correctly.

1. Beam me up Scotty!

____

2. Well Bones what is your diagnosis?

____

3. Mr. Sulu go to Warp 5.

____

4. If it weren't for you Spock there'd be no aliens aboard.

____

5. Why do we have to wear these funny clothes Captain?

____

ANSWERS 1. Popeye, 2. , Indiana Jones 3. , Dr. Welby, 4. Members of the jury, 5. , Perry Mason,

PUNCTUATING

Commas with nouns of address

If you need help using commas with nouns of address, turn to Punctuation Rule 9 on page 122.

On the lines below, rewrite the story given on the right. Be sure to punctuate the nouns of address correctly.

Last night on The Tonight Show, Johnny Carson welcomed several famous guests. "Tonight folks we are pleased to present George Washington, his mother, and Clark Kent. Mr. Kent let's begin with you. Can you tell us something about your background sir?"

"Well Johnny I had a super boyhood. Maybe my background was something like yours Mr. Washington. George do you remember leaping tall buildings in a single bound on your farm?"

"What I most remember Mr. Kent is chopping down trees. What do you remember Mother?"

"Mostly Son I remember baking hundreds of cherry pies. Believe me Johnny it isn't easy being the grandmother of our country."

PUNCTUATING

Commas with appositives

If you need help using commas with appositives, turn to Punctuation Rule 10 on page 122.

PRECHECK. In each sentence below, find the appositive. Then write it on the line next to the sentence. Be sure to include the comma or commas that belong with it. Check your answers at the bottom of the page.

1. Mac Norton the Human Aquarium swallowed 24 live frogs. ____________________
2. Richebourg a two-foot-tall spy disguised himself as a baby. ____________________
3. A famous dentist was Doc Holliday a gunslinger. ____________________
4. In 1923, Walt Disney the cartoonist went bankrupt. ____________________
5. In Oz, Dorothy wore magic shoes the ruby slippers. ____________________

Number right: ______ *If less than 5, review the rule in the Reference Guide.*

Rewrite the following sentences. Be sure to punctuate the appositives correctly.

1. Turn On a TV comedy series was cancelled after one day.

   ____

2. Alfonso the Man with the Ostrich Stomach ate glass.

   ____

3. President Nixon had a famous dog Checkers.

   ____

4. Packy East a boxer is better known as Bob Hope.

   ____

5. Fans still visit Elvis's estate Graceland.

   ____

ANSWERS 1. , the Human Aquarium, 2. , a two-foot-tall spy, 3. , a gunslinger 4. , the cartoonist, 5. , the ruby slippers

PUNCTUATING

Commas with appositives

If you need help using commas with appositives, turn to Punctuation Rule 10 on page 122.

The paragraph below this list is missing appositives. Use the items in the list to help you complete the paragraph. Be sure to punctuate the appositives correctly.

American Sign Language—a language used by deaf people
Arlecchino—a dog
Jaco—a parrot in Austria
Washoe's friends—other chimpanzees
Chris—another mongrel
Kampala—the capital of Uganda
Washoe—a chimpanzee
Benjy—a mongrel dog
A Russian stallion—Clever Hans
Lady Wonder—a horse

Some animals can almost talk. For instance, Arlecchino ______________ learned to type with his nose. On TV, "Raindrops Keep Fallin' on My Head" was sung by Benjy ________________ ____________. Chris ______________________________ could predict the winners of horse races. Lady Wonder _________________ could both type and predict the future. People were also amazed by a Russian stallion ______________________ who supposedly could do arithmetic. Many parrots can speak, but Jaco _________________ _________________ seemed to know what he was saying. Near Kampala ___________________________________ people were upset by an angry tortoise who demanded to see the police commissioner. Perhaps the most famous talking animal is Washoe _________________________. She uses American Sign Language ____ to talk to people. Washoe is now teaching her friends _______________ _________________________ to use sign language, too. So someday, a chimp may walk up to you and ask for directions.

PUNCTUATING

Commas with appositives

If you need help using commas with appositives, turn to Punctuation Rule 10 on page 122.

On the lines below, rewrite the paragraph given on the right. Be sure to punctuate the appositives correctly.

Many famous people got their start in football. Eisenhower, Nixon, and Ford three recent presidents played football in college. The young Nixon a reserve tackle sat on the bench most of the time. Ford a center at the University of Michigan even got pro offers from two teams the Chicago Bears and the Detroit Lions. Johnny Mack Brown a cowboy hero in the movies was an All-American halfback at the University of Alabama. "Whizzer" White a player with the Pittsburgh Pirates and the Detroit Lions later became known as Byron White a Supreme Court justice. Kris Kristofferson the actor and country-western singer was right at home in Semi-Tough a movie about football. He had been a football star at Pomona College a small college in California.

Writing Activity 5 *If you need help, refer to the rules noted on pages 56–66 and 69–71.*

You are building a house. Rain is expected soon, and you need to finish the job fast. Fill in the blanks below.

You already have some people helping you:

Jake, a carpenter, is helping you;
Pam, an electrician, is helping you;
Sandy, a painter, is helping you.

Who else would you ask to help? (Use appositives, as above.)

Which four rooms still need to be finished? (List them in the order in which you would finish them.)

What jobs still need to be done in these rooms?

What three things would you do to celebrate the end of the project?

Now write a paragraph about the house you are building. Include the information you have just given. Use some compound sentences, series, introductory phrases and clauses, and appositives.

PUNCTUATING

Commas or exclamation points with interjections

If you need help using commas or exclamation points with interjections, turn to Punctuation Rule 11 on page 122.

PRECHECK. Find the interjection in each item below. Then, on the line next to the item, write the interjection with the correct punctuation. Check your answers at the bottom of the page.

1. Hey Jude! ____________________
2. Shh No talking! ____________________
3. Darn I shouldn't have hired Dracula to work at the blood bank. ____________________
4. Well guess who's coming to dinner? ____________________
5. Golly gee Grandpa, why can't we talk like everyone else? ____________________

Number right: _____ *If less than 5, review the rule in the Reference Guide.*

The following dialogue is missing interjections. Fill in the blanks with interjections from the list on the left below. Use each interjection at least once. Be sure to punctuate the interjections correctly.

Hey
Well
Wow
Gee
Oh

"__________ I bet you think that basketball players just play basketball all day."

"__________ I wouldn't say that."

"__________ one time Clifford Ray of the Golden State Warriors helped remove some metal that a 350-pound dolphin had swallowed."

"__________ why was he asked to help?"

"__________ his arms are three feet, nine inches long."

"__________"

ANSWERS 1. Hey, 2. Shh! 3. Darn! 4. Well, 5. Golly gee,

PUNCTUATING

Commas or exclamation points with interjections

If you need help using commas or exclamation points with interjections, turn to Punctuation Rule 11 on page 122.

Rewrite the sentences below. Be sure to punctuate the interjections correctly.

1. Oh Grandma, what big eyes you have!

   ____

2. Ouch I can't believe I ate the whole thing.

   ____

3. Yuck Sally just put peanut butter on her eggs.

   ____

4. Ah I love the taste of chocolate first thing in the morning.

   ____

5. Gosh Toto, I don't think we're in Kansas anymore.

   ____

6. Wow That's incredible!

   ____

7. Well tell us about your exercise program, Mr. T.

   ____

8. Hey have you met Rosemary's baby?

   ____

9. Darn My toe is caught in the bathtub faucet.

   ____

10. Hurrah I'm finished.

    ____

PUNCTUATING

Commas after greetings in friendly letters

If you need help with commas after greetings in friendly letters, turn to Punctuation Rule 12 on page 122.

The greetings for some friendly letters are given below. Rewrite them on the lines that follow. Be sure to punctuate them correctly.

Dear Abby

Dear Ann

Dear Dad

Dear Aunt Bea

Dear Uncle Ben

Dear Mr. Ree

Dear Mutt and Jeff

Dear Mrs. Olson

Dear Minnie

Dear Mr. Whipple

Dear Miss Rule

Dear Peter

Dear Cousin Amy

Dear John

Dear Ms. Tree

Dear Dr. Jekyll

Dear Mr. Hyde

Dear Grandma

Dear Miss Piggy

Dear Mr. Science

Dear Mom

Now write three greetings of your own.

PUNCTUATING

Commas after closings in friendly letters and business letters

If you need help with commas after closings in friendly letters and business letters, turn to Punctuation Rule 13 on page 122.

The closings in some friendly letters and business letters are given below. Rewrite them on the lines that follow. Be sure to punctuate them correctly.

Very truly yours
Sandy Beach

____

____

Yours truly
Julio Gallo

____

____

Very truly yours
D. Light

____

____

Love
Bonnie and Clyde

____

____

Sincerely
Juan Valdez

____

____

Sincerely yours
Orville Redenbacher

____

____

Your friend
Flicka

____

____

Yours sincerely
Pat T. Kake

____

____

Love
Grandma

____

____

Fondly
Aunt Polly

____

____

Sincerely
Barb E. Dahl

____

____

Yours truly
Dan D. Lyon

____

____

Writing Activity 6

If you need help, refer to the rules noted on pages 74–77.

Here is the start of a friendly letter. Finish the letter on the lines below. Use at least two interjections. Don't forget to supply an opening and closing in the letter.

April 1, 1988

____

You'll never believe what happened in my science class today! We were all taking a test when one of the lab animals got out. Well, the test ended right then. What started was much more interesting.

PUNCTUATING

Quotation marks with direct quotations

If you need help using quotation marks with direct quotations, turn to Punctuation Rule 14 on page 122.

PRECHECK. The sentences below are missing quotation marks. Rewrite the sentences on the lines that follow. Be sure to use quotation marks with any direct quotations you find. Check your answers at the bottom of the page.

1. Leo Durocher said, Nice guys finish last.

   ____

2. In his first play, Humphrey Bogart asked, Tennis, anyone?

   ____

3. You can't, Thomas Wolfe claimed, go home again.

   ____

4. Go ahead. Make my day, Clint Eastwood said.

   ____

5. President Truman said, The buck stops here.

   ____

6. P. T. Barnum said, There's a sucker born every minute.

   ____

7. F. Scott Fitzgerald said, The rich are different from us.

   ____

8. Hemingway replied, Yes, they have more money.

   ____

Number right: _____ *If less than 8, review the rule in the Reference Guide.*

ANSWERS 1. Leo Durocher said, "Nice guys finish last." 2. In his first play, Humphrey Bogart asked, "Tennis, anyone?" 3. "You can't," Thomas Wolfe claimed, "go home again." 4. "Go ahead. Make my day," Clint Eastwood said. 5. President Truman said, "The buck stops here." 6. P. T. Barnum said, "There's a sucker born every minute." 7. F. Scott Fitzgerald said, "The rich are different from us." 8. Hemingway replied, "Yes, they have more money."

PUNCTUATING

Quotation marks with direct quotations

If you need help using quotation marks with direct quotations, turn to Punctuation Rule 14 on page 122.

The sentences below are missing quotation marks. Rewrite the sentences on the lines that follow. Be sure to use quotation marks with any direct quotations you find.

1. Will Rogers said, I never met a man I didn't like.

   ____

2. All politics is applesauce, he also said.

   ____

3. Peel me a grape, Mae West said.

   ____

4. A tie, Bear Bryant claimed, is like kissing your sister.

   ____

5. I want to be alone, Greta Garbo said.

   ____

6. Knute Rockne told his team, Win one for the Gipper.

   ____

7. Here's looking at you, kid, Humphrey Bogart said.

   ____

8. He <u>didn't</u> say, Play it again, Sam.

   ____

9. The game's not over, Yogi Berra said, till it's over.

   ____

10. Oliver Twist said, Please, Sir, I want some more.

    ____

PUNCTUATING

Quotation marks with direct quotations

If you need help using quotation marks with direct quotations, turn to Punctuation Rule 14 on page 122.

The stories below contain direct quotations. Rewrite the conversations on the lines that follow. Be sure to put quotation marks around the direct quotations. You don't need to copy the parts before the conversations begin.

The following conversation took place in the movie Silk Stockings.

I just got your call, one character said. I—I was having a manicure.

The other asked, At two o'clock in the morning?

I cannot sleep with long fingernails, the first person answered.

Baseball players Dizzy Dean and his brother Daffy were taking a train ride. Just before they came to a tunnel, Daffy opened a soda.

Diz, Daffy asked, you tried any of this stuff?

Just fixin' to, his brother answered. Why?

Don't! replied Daffy. I did, and I've gone plumb blind.

PUNCTUATING

Quotation marks with direct quotations

If you need help using quotation marks with direct quotations, turn to Punctuation Rule 14 on page 122.

On the lines below, rewrite the paragraph given on the right. Be sure to put quotation marks around any direct quotations you find.

Coaches sometimes joke about being fired. For instance, when he was leaving the Denver Broncos, John Ralston said, I left because of illness and fatigue. The fans were sick and tired of me. One college football coach told why he didn't ask for a lifetime contract. I had a friend with a lifetime contract, Bob Devaney said. After two bad years, the university president called him into his office and pronounced him dead. Another college coach said he was happy to leave his job. I'm going to become a hog farmer, Al Conover stated. After some of the things I've been through, I regard it as a step up.

PUNCTUATING

Commas with direct quotations

If you need help using commas with direct quotations, turn to Punctuation Rule 15 on page 122.

PRECHECK. **The sentences below are missing commas. Rewrite the sentences on the lines that follow. Be sure to use commas with any direct quotations you find. Check your answers at the bottom of the page.**

1. "The bigger they are" a boxer said "the harder they fall."

   ____

2. Another boxer said "I zigged when I should have zagged."

   ____

3. "When the going gets tough" Rockne said "the tough get going."

   ____

4. "Elementary" said Sherlock Holmes.

   ____

5. Edward Albee said "Never give a sucker an even break."

   ____

6. "You're a mouse studying to be a rat" Wilson Mizner said.

   ____

7. "I shall return" Douglas MacArthur promised.

   ____

Number right: ______ *If less than 7, review the rule in the Reference Guide.*

ANSWERS 1. "The bigger they are," a boxer said, "the harder they fall." 2. Another boxer said, "I zigged when I should have zagged." 3. "When the going gets tough," Rockne said, "the tough get going." 4. "Elementary," said Sherlock Holmes. 5. Edward Albee said, "Never give a sucker an even break." 6. "You're a mouse studying to be a rat," Wilson Mizner said. 7. "I shall return," Douglas MacArthur promised.

PUNCTUATING

Commas with direct quotations

If you need help using commas with direct quotations, turn to Punctuation Rule 15 on page 122.

The sentences below are missing commas. Rewrite the sentences on the lines that follow. Be sure to use commas with any direct quotations you find.

1. "Mom always liked you best" Tommy said.

   ____

2. She complained "You never want a second cup at home."

   ____

3. "Mrs. Olson's coffee" he replied "is the richest kind."

   ____

4. "You deserve a break today" the gangster said.

   ____

5. Sam Goldwyn said "I read part of it all the way through."

   ____

6. He also said "I would be sticking my head in a moose."

   ____

7. "Marry the boss's daughter" Robert Rogers advised.

   ____

8. The cowboy said "I want to die with my boots on."

   ____

9. "That" the teacher said "is not how you spell <u>relief</u>."

   ____

10. Soldiers often hear "Hurry up and wait."

   ____

PUNCTUATING

Commas with direct quotations

If you need help using commas with direct quotations, turn to Punctuation Rule 15 on page 122.

The stories below contain direct quotations. Rewrite the conversations on the lines that follow. Be sure to include any missing commas. You don't need to copy the parts before the conversations begin.

John Drew, an Atlanta Hawks forward, was talking to a secretary. She was helping him fill out some forms.

The secretary asked "What's your birth date, John?"

"September 30" he answered.

She asked "What year?"

"Every year" he said.

The Beatles were about to record a record. The producer, George Martin, was telling them what he wanted to do.

Martin said "Let me know if there's anything you don't like."

"Well, for a start" George Harrison replied "I don't like your tie."

PUNCTUATING

Commas with direct quotations

If you need help using commas with direct quotations, turn to Punctuation Rule 15 on page 122.

On the lines below, rewrite the paragraph given on the right. Be sure to put in any missing commas.

Movies and sports often give us funny insults. In the movie Make Way for Tomorrow, a father told his son "Don't think too hard, Robert. You might hurt yourself." Once pitcher Jerry Reuss saw a radio announcer who was wearing a yellow shirt and red pants. "Why don't you buy a green hat" he asked "and hire out as a traffic signal?" Sometimes people insult themselves. "It took me 17 years to get 3,000 hits in baseball. I did it in one afternoon on the golf course" baseball great Hank Aaron said. When a middle-aged woman in California Suite was looking in the mirror at her wrinkles, she said "I look like a brand-new steel-belted radial tire."

PUNCTUATING

End punctuation with direct quotations

If you need help using end punctuation with direct quotations, turn to Punctuation Rule 16 on page 123.

PRECHECK. The following sentences contain direct quotations that are missing their end punctuation. On the line next to each sentence, write the last word in the quotation, the end punctuation mark, and the closing quotation marks. Check your answers at the bottom of the page.

1. "I am the greatest" Muhammad Ali exclaimed. ____________________
2. The movie star said, "My face is my fortune" ____________________
3. The children shouted, "Ring around the collar" ____________________
4. Clara asked, "Where's the beef" ____________________
5. Ben Franklin said, "There never was a good war or a bad peace" ____________________

Number right: _____ *If less than 5, review the rule in the Reference Guide.*

The following sentences contain direct quotations that are missing their end punctuation. On the line next to each sentence, write the last word in the quotation, the end punctuation mark, and the closing quotation marks.

1. Lee said, "Cats work in the English post office" ____________________
2. "Do they deliver mail" May asked. ____________________
3. "Of course not" he exclaimed. ____________________
4. She asked, "Well, what do they do, then" ____________________
5. Lee said, "They catch mice" ____________________
6. "Do they get paid" May asked. ____________________
7. "Yes. They even get veterinary insurance" he exclaimed. ____________________

ANSWERS 1. greatest!" 2. fortune." 3. collar!" 4. beef?" 5. peace."

PUNCTUATING

End punctuation with direct quotations

If you need help using end punctuation with direct quotations, turn to Punctuation Rule 16 on page 123.

Rewrite the sentences below. Be sure to supply the correct end punctuation for any direct quotations.

1. She claimed, "Donald Duck is a famous hero"

2. "Do you expect me to believe that" he asked.

3. She said, "It's true. He saved a city's water supply"

4. "Oh, come on" he exclaimed.

5. She explained, "A ship sank with 6,000 sheep aboard"

6. "Did the dead sheep pollute the water" he asked.

7. She said, "They would have. But a comic book saved the day"

8. He asked, "Was it the one about the Ping-Pong balls"

9. "Yes. How did you know" she asked.

10. He said, "Donald used Ping-Pong balls to raise a ship"

11. She said, "That's what was done to raise this ship, too"

PUNCTUATING

End punctuation with direct quotations

If you need help using end punctuation with direct quotations, turn to Punctuation Rule 16 on page 123.

On the lines below, rewrite the paragraph given on the right. Be sure to supply the correct end punctuation for any direct quotations you find.

Sports figures often entertain us off the field as well as on. Baseball manager Casey Stengel said, "The secret of managing a club is to keep the five guys who hate you away from the five who are undecided" Once Joel Horlen was asked what he threw to a batter who hit a home run. He replied, "It was a baseball" When Babe Ruth was stopped for driving the wrong way on a one-way street, he exclaimed, "I'm only drivin' one way" Dizzy Dean wondered, "It puzzles me how they know what corners are good for filling stations" Then he went on to ask, "Just how did these fellows know there was gas and oil under here"

Writing Activity 7

If you need help, refer to the rules noted on pages 79–89.

Part of a conversation between two brothers is given on the right. Continue the conversation on the lines below. Remember to punctuate the direct quotations correctly and to start a new paragraph each time you change speakers.

"Ed," Harry said, "you sure look nice tonight."

"What do you want?" Ed replied.

"Funny you should ask," said Harry. "I sort of have a problem. Some guys I know are getting a football game together on Saturday."

"Oh, so you want me to be quarterback?" Ed asked.

"Not exactly," Harry laughed. "Not unless you want to call plays for the lawn mower."

"What's that supposed to mean?" asked Ed.

"Well, I promised Mom that I'd mow the lawn and wash the car on Saturday," Harry explained. "But now I want to play in the game instead. I thought maybe you could do the jobs for me."

"Well, maybe I could," Ed said. "But it'll cost you."

"I figured that," Harry answered. "What do you want in return?"

Edna and Bill have come to Jack's house to complain about his loud party. Look at the picture on the right and make up a conversation between Edna, Bill, and Jack. Then write the conversation on the lines below. Remember to punctuate the direct quotations correctly and to start a new paragraph each time you change speakers.

PUNCTUATING

Quotation marks with titles of works
Underlines with titles of works

If you need help using quotation marks and underlines with titles of works, turn to Punctuation Rules 17 and 18 on page 123.

PRECHECK. Each of the following sentences contains a title. On the line next to the sentence, write the title correctly. Be sure either to underline the title or to put quotation marks around it. Check your answers at the bottom of the page.

1. A woman wrote the oldest novel, The Tale of Genji. ____________________
2. The Star-Spangled Banner was composed on an envelope. ____________________
3. Richard and Pat Nixon acted in a play, The Dark Tower. ____________________
4. The essay A Modest Proposal suggests that we eat babies. ____________________
5. There was once a TV puppet show called Rootie Kazootie. ____________________

Number right: _____ *If less than 5, review the rules in the Reference Guide.*

PUNCTUATING

Quotation marks with titles of works

Find the titles in the sentences below. Then write the titles on the lines next to the sentences. Be sure to put quotation marks around the titles.

1. Ogden Nash called a poem I Do, I Will, I Have. ____________________
2. Suwannee River is Florida's state song. ____________________
3. Uncle Creepy was introduced in the story Monster Rally. ____________________
4. Connecticut's state song is Yankee Doodle. ____________________
5. Pig and Pepper is a chapter in Alice in Wonderland. ____________________
6. Kipling's poem If has been translated into 27 languages. ____________________
7. Milton's Areopagitica is a very famous essay. ____________________

ANSWERS 1. The Tale of Genji 2. "The Star-Spangled Banner" 3. The Dark Tower 4. "A Modest Proposal" 5. Rootie Kazootie

PUNCTUATING

Quotation marks with titles of works

If you need help using quotation marks with titles of works, turn to Punctuation Rule 17 on page 123.

On the lines below, rewrite the paragraph given on the right. Be sure to put quotation marks around any story, song, and poem titles you find.

Children often like to try to scare each other. When you were a child, maybe you sang either I Want a Bowl of Greasy, Grimy Gopher Guts or The Worms Crawl In, the Worms Crawl Out. Perhaps you were scared by the Headless Horseman in the story The Legend of Sleepy Hollow. Both children and adults have been frightened by the living corpse in the story The Monkey's Paw. The burning of Sam's body in the poem The Cremation of Sam McGee is also frightening. One of the masters of horror is Edgar Allan Poe. In his story The Black Cat, a black cat pursues a murderer to his death. In The Tell-Tale Heart, a murderer is haunted by the beating of his victim's heart. The Pit and the Pendulum tells the story of a swinging blade coming closer and closer to a man in a pit.

PUNCTUATING

Underlines with titles of works

If you need help using underlines with titles of works, turn to Punctuation Rule 18 on page 123.

In the sentences below, find the titles that should be underlined. Write the titles correctly on the lines next to the sentences.

1. The first crossword puzzle was in St. Nicholas magazine. ____________________
2. The novel Gone with the Wind sold 1,500,000 copies in a year. ____________________
3. On the TV show Bonanza, Hoss's horse was called Chub. ____________________
4. The horror movie Macabre was shown in a cemetery. ____________________
5. The play The Warp is over 18 hours long. ____________________
6. The newspaper Clark Kent works for is the Daily Planet. ____________________

Rewrite the sentences below. Be sure to underline any titles of works you find.

1. The Green Hornet published the newspaper the Daily Sentinel.

   ____

   ____

2. James Thurber wrote a book called Let Your Mind Alone.

   ____

3. A scene in the movie 2001 was filmed in a corset factory.

   ____

4. Agatha Christie's play The Mousetrap ran for 30 years.

   ____

5. Bill Cosby once starred in the TV show I Spy.

   ____

PUNCTUATING

Underlines with titles of works

If you need help using underlines with titles of works, turn to Punctuation Rule 18 on page 123.

On the lines below, rewrite the paragraph given on the right. Be sure to underline the titles of TV shows and movies.

Many famous movie stars were once known for their TV roles. For instance, Sally Field was Sister Bertrille in the TV show The Flying Nun. Later, she starred in the movies Norma Rae and Places in the Heart. People once thought of Cher as a hippie singer on the TV series The Sonny and Cher Show. They were surprised at how well she acted in the movies Silkwood and Mask. John Travolta first appeared as a high school student in the TV show Welcome Back, Kotter. He became more famous in the movies Saturday Night Fever and Urban Cowboy. Eddie Murphy got his start on the TV show Saturday Night Live. Later, he starred in the movies Trading Places and Beverly Hills Cop.

PUNCTUATING

Apostrophes in contractions

If you need help with apostrophes in contractions, turn to Punctuation Rule 19 on page 123.

PRECHECK. In each sentence below, find the contraction that is missing its apostrophe. Then write the contraction correctly on the line next to the sentence. Check your answers at the bottom of the page.

1. Theres honey at the center of golf balls. ____________
2. Dolly Partons only five feet tall. ____________
3. We dont sleep as much as our ancestors did. ____________
4. A person's hair cant really turn white overnight. ____________
5. According to one scientist, were very much like ants. ____________

Number right: ____ *If less than 5, review the rule in the Reference Guide.*

Rewrite the sentences below. Be sure to include the apostrophes in the contractions.

1. Surely youve read about the fate of many mummies.
2. No, I havent.
3. Well, bit by bit theyve been swallowed.
4. Youre kidding!
5. Its hard to believe, but mummy powder was once a medicine.

ANSWERS 1. There's 2. Parton's 3. don't 4. can't 5. we're

PUNCTUATING

Apostrophes in contractions

If you need help with apostrophes in contractions, turn to Punctuation Rule 19 on page 123.

The paragraphs below are missing some contractions. Use the words in the parentheses to form each contraction. Write the contractions on the writing lines. Don't forget the apostrophes.

Maybe (you have) ________________ heard stories of children who were raised by wild animals. (Tarzan is) ________________ famous for having lived with apes. (There is) ________________ also the story of Mowgli, an Indian boy (who is) ________________ raised by wolves. These stories (are not) ________________ really true. But we (can not) ________________ be sure about some of the others.

(India is) ________________ the source of many of these stories. Some Indians (do not) ________________ believe in killing wolves. (They have) ________________ also sometimes left unwanted girl babies to die in the jungle. (It is) ________________ possible that some of these babies (could have) ________________ been raised by wolves. For instance, two Indian girls were found in a wolf den. No one knew how long (they had) ________________ lived there. They (could not) ________________ walk, talk, or stand. (They had) ________________ developed wolflike habits. (They had) ________________ learned to walk on all fours, to bark, and to sleep huddled together. They (were not) ________________ interested in other people, but they did like dogs.

One girl died before (she had) ________________ learned to see herself as human. The other girl did learn to speak and to see herself as human, but she (was not) ________________ ever able to communicate fully.

PUNCTUATING

Apostrophes in contractions

If you need help with apostrophes in contractions, turn to Punctuation Rule 19 on page 123.

On the lines below, rewrite the paragraph given on the right. Be sure to put apostrophes in the contractions.

There are few baseball fans whod deny that Ted Williams was one of the greatest baseball players of all time. Hes best known as a hitter. His 1941 batting average of .406 hasnt been beaten since then. Theres one story about him that few people know. In 1959, hed earned $125,000 from the Boston Red Sox, but hed batted only .254. Before that year, hed always batted at least .300. The Red Sox offered him the same salary the next year, but he didnt want that. He said that, since he hadnt played well, he shouldnt get that much money. He wouldnt sign the contract unless his salary was cut $35,000. Its a rare person who asks for a salary cut!

PUNCTUATING

Apostrophes in possessive nouns

If you need help with apostrophes in possessive nouns, turn to Punctuation Rule 20 on page 123.

PRECHECK. In each sentence below, find the possessive noun that is missing its apostrophe. Then write the noun correctly on the line next to the sentence. Check your answers at the bottom of the page.

1. In Bonanza, Little Joes horse is Cochise. ________________
2. One of Thailands sports is kite fighting. ________________
3. The Three Musketeers motto is "All for one, one for all." ________________
4. Butch Cassidys real name was Robert Leroy Parker. ________________
5. Peoples brains have been getting heavier. ________________

Number right: ______ *If less than 5, review the rule in the Reference Guide.*

Rewrite the sentences below. Be sure to put apostrophes in the possessive nouns.

1. Abraham Lincolns brothers-in-law fought for the South.

____

2. Mens hearing is not as good as womens.

____

3. Teddy Roosevelts mother and wife died on the same day.

____

4. A persons skin weighs about six pounds.

____

5. Hurricanes names are both male and female.

____

ANSWERS 1. Joe's 2. Thailand's 3. Musketeers' 4. Cassidy's 5. People's

PUNCTUATING

Apostrophes in possessive nouns

If you need help with apostrophes in possessive nouns, turn to Punctuation Rule 20 on page 123.

The paragraph below is missing some possessive nouns. Use the words in the parentheses to form the possessive nouns. Write the possessive nouns on the writing lines. Don't forget the apostrophes.

You can sometimes tell something about (someones) ________________ personality by the way he or she looks. For example, my friend (Moonbeams) ________________ hair is long. Her (jeans) ________________ knees are patched, and her sandal straps are broken. (Moonbeams) ________________ clothing and love beads tell people she is a hippie. (Chads) ________________ clothes tell a different story. His (polo shirts) ________________ emblems make it clear that he is a preppy. He wears his (grandfathers) ________________ watch and spends his (fathers) ________________ money. Another one of my friends is Moose, who is the football (teams) ________________ star tackle. (Mooses) ________________ favorite outfit is jeans, a ripped football jersey, and sneakers. His (noses) ________________ odd shape comes from its having been broken three times. (Sidneys) ________________ style is the oddest. His best (friends) ________________ name for him is "Dead Rat." His (Mohawks) ________________ purple spikes stand straight up. To his (parents) ________________ surprise, Sidney wears a safety pin through his nose on special occasions.

PUNCTUATING

Apostrophes in possessive nouns

If you need help with apostrophes in possessive nouns, turn to Punctuation Rule 20 on page 123.

Rewrite the sentences below. Be sure to put apostrophes in the possessive nouns.

1. A wallet makers decision once caused problems.

   ____

2. In each wallets main compartment, the maker put a card.

   ____

3. The cards appearance was that of a Social Security card.

   ____

4. On the card, the maker put his secretarys Social Security number.

   ____

5. Some of the wallets buyers thought the number was theirs.

   ____

6. These peoples Social Security taxes went to that account.

   ____

7. Thousands of dollars were paid into that numbers account.

   ____

8. The government decided to change the secretarys number.

   ____

9. So now the government workers worries about the secretarys account are over.

   ____

   ____

10. But how will they trace the wallet buyers taxes that went into the wrong account?

    ____

    ____

PUNCTUATING

Apostrophes in possessive nouns

If you need help with apostrophes in possessive nouns, turn to Punctuation Rule 20 on page 123.

On the lines below, rewrite the paragraph given on the right. Be sure to put apostrophes in the possessive nouns.

Peoples mistakes are often embarrassing, especially when they happen in public. For instance, Dan O'Learys home run didn't help his team. The umpires decision was that O'Leary was out because he had run around the bases the wrong way. Some peoples mistakes are more serious. A judges error put a man in jail for 21 years. Paul Huberts crime was supposed to be murder. Hubert was freed when his victims name was found out. He had been jailed for killing himself. The governments mistakes can sometimes be funny. Once, the U.S. Mints workers put the wrong words on some gold coins. The coins words should have been "In God We Trust"; but instead, they were "In Gold We Trust."

PUNCTUATING

Colons after greetings in business letters

If you need help with colons after greetings in business letters, turn to Punctuation Rule 21 on page 123.

The greetings for some business letters are given on the right and below. Rewrite them on the lines that follow. Be sure to punctuate them correctly.

Dear Miss Brooks

Dear Colonel Sanders

Dear Judge Parker

Dear Mr. President

To Whom It May Concern

Dear Representative Case

Dear General Grant

Dear Nurse Barton

Dear Dr. Frankenstein

Dear Mrs. Windsor

Dear Professor Higgins

Dear Senator Lee

Dear Mr. Kellogg

Gentlemen

Dear Ms. Steinem

Sir

Dear Dr. No

Dear Mrs. Gomez

Madam

Dear Mr. Aoki

Writing Activity 8

If you need help, refer to the rules noted on pages 96–103.

Two weeks ago you bought a television set. Since then, several things have gone wrong with it. You decide to write a letter to the store to complain. Before you write the letter, you take some notes. Fill in the blanks below.

Date of purchase: ____________________

Store where the TV set was bought: Sam's TV Mart

Store's Owner: Samuel R. Phibbs

What's gone wrong with the TV:

The set's knobs stick.

The picture isn't sharp.

____

____

What I've done so far:

I've called the store's repairperson, but no one has come.

I tried to return the TV set, but the store wouldn't take it back.

____

____

What I now expect the store to do:

____

____

____

____

____

____

____

____

____

____

Write a business letter complaining to the store's owner. Include the information you have noted on page 104. Use some contractions and some possessive nouns. Don't forget the opening and the closing of the letter.

(Date)

PUNCTUATING

Colons in expressions of time

If you need help with colons in expressions of time, turn to Punctuation Rule 22 on page 123.

PRECHECK. Find the expressions of time in the sentences below. Then write them on the lines next to the sentences. Be sure to include the colons. Check your answers at the bottom of the page.

1. The first test-tube baby was born at 1147 P.M. ________________
2. Charles Lindbergh landed in Paris at 1021 P.M. ________________
3. At 256 A.M., a man set foot on the moon. ________________
4. The president's term ends at 1200 noon on January 20. ________________

Number right: _____ *If less than 4, review the rule in the Reference Guide.*

Rewrite the sentences below. Make sure you put colons in the expressions of time.

1. In 1943 in South Dakota, it was –4° F at 730 A.M.

   ____

2. At 732 A.M. the same day, it was +45° F.

   ____

3. At 902 A.M. in 1896, Britain and Zanzibar went to war.

   ____

4. By 940 A.M. on the same day, the war was over.

   ____

5. A boxing match started at 915 P.M. in 1893.

   ____

6. It ended 110 rounds later, at 434 A.M. the next day.

   ____

ANSWERS 1. 11:47 P.M. 2. 10:21 P.M. 3. 2:56 A.M. 4. 12:00 noon

PUNCTUATING

Hyphens in numbers and fractions

If you need help with hyphens in numbers and fractions, turn to Punctuation Rule 23 on page 123.

PRECHECK. In the sentences below, find the numbers and fractions that should have hyphens. Then write them correctly on the lines next to the sentences. Check your answers at the bottom of the page.

1. A couple rode a Ferris wheel for thirty seven days. ____________
2. A giant squid's eye can be one and one fourth feet wide. ____________
3. Steak is seventy four percent water. ____________
4. A woman weighed seven and one half pounds. ____________
5. A boy created a house of cards sixty eight stories tall. ____________

Number right: _____ *If less than 5, review the rule in the Reference Guide.*

In the sentences below, find the numbers and fractions that should have hyphens. Then write them correctly on the lines next to the sentences.

1. Reggie Jackson's bat weighs two and one quarter pounds. ____________
2. A hockey puck weighs about one third pound. ____________
3. A gold bar at Fort Knox weighs over twenty seven pounds. ____________
4. A man's brain weighs three and one tenth pounds. ____________
5. The comic strip "Blondie" is printed in fifty five nations. ____________
6. An ostrich egg can weigh thirty one pounds. ____________
7. A crocodile twenty seven feet long weighed 4,400 pounds. ____________

ANSWERS 1. thirty-seven 2. one-fourth 3. seventy-four 4. one-half 5. sixty-eight

PUNCTUATING

Hyphens in numbers and fractions

If you need help with hyphens in numbers and fractions, turn to Punctuation Rule 23 on page 123.

On the lines below, rewrite the paragraph given on the right. Be sure to put the missing hyphens in the numbers and fractions.

It seems there is a record for everything. Did you know, for instance, that the largest bubble blown with bubble gum was twenty one inches wide? People have finished a bathtub race thirty six miles long in under one and one half hours. Someone balanced on one foot for thirty three hours. And someone else played an accordion nonstop for eighty four hours. A man stood 169,713 dominoes on end in a row that was four and one third miles long. When he toppled them, they fell at a speed of two and one quarter miles per hour. One man ate twenty and three fourths hamburgers in one half hour. They each weighed three and one half ounces. I think I'd rather become famous in some other way!

POSTTEST

Each sentence below has some words or punctuation marks left out. From the lettered choices that follow the sentence, choose the one that will complete the sentence correctly. Then fill in the oval next to the correct letter.

Capitalization

1. I've always wanted to see ___.

   0 A. buckingham palace
   0 B. Buckingham palace
   0 C. buckingham Palace
   0 D. Buckingham Palace

2. Many people consider ___ the end of summer.

   0 A. labor day
   0 B. Labor Day
   0 C. labor Day
   0 D. Labor day

3. I watched the old movie ___ on TV last night.

   0 A. Around the World in Eighty Days
   0 B. Around The World In Eighty Days
   0 C. Around the world in eighty days
   0 D. around the World in Eighty Days

4. On his vacation, he went to ___.

   0 A. Paris, Texas
   0 B. paris, texas
   0 C. Paris, texas
   0 D. paris, Texas

5. I opened the door and shouted, ___

   0 A. "Is Anyone Home?"
   0 B. "Is anyone home?"
   0 C. "is anyone home?"
   0 D. "is anyone Home?"

6. My appointment with ___ is at two o'clock.

   0 A. DR. Shaw
   0 B. dr. Shaw
   0 C. Dr. Shaw
   0 D. dR. Shaw

7. I got my new puppy at the ___

   0 A. S.p.c.a.
   0 B. s.p.c.a.
   0 C. S.P.C.A.
   0 D. S.p.C.a.

Punctuation

1. I wanted to go to the party ___ I had to work late.

   0 A. , but,
   0 B. but,
   0 C. , but
   0 D. but

2. He said, ___

   0 A. Your socks are on the wrong feet.
   0 B. "Your socks are on the wrong feet.
   0 C. Your socks are on the wrong feet."
   0 D. "Your socks are on the wrong feet."

3. I asked him if he liked his new job ___

   0 A. . (period)
   0 B. ? (question mark)
   0 C. ! (exclamation point)
   0 D. , (comma)

4. The three ___ suits were all the same.

○ A. mens
○ B. men's
○ C. mens'
○ D. mans'

5. Tell me ___ how is Archie these days?

○ A. Edith
○ B. , Edith
○ C. , Edith,
○ D. Edith,

6. ___ "you should go home now."

○ A. "I think" she said
○ B. "I think" she said,
○ C. "I think," she said,
○ D. "I think," she said

7. I saw Jean ___ at the movie.

○ A. , the girl in the plaid sneakers,
○ B. the girl in the plaid sneakers
○ C. the girl in the plaid sneakers,
○ D. , the girl in the plaid sneakers

8. I ___ realize it was so late.

○ A. did'nt
○ B. didnt
○ C. didn't
○ D. did n't

9. Singing ___ did not end the dry spell.

○ A. "<u>Raindrops Keep Fallin' on My Head</u>"
○ B. Raindrops Keep Fallin' on My Head
○ C. "Raindrops Keep Fallin' on My Head
○ D. "Raindrops Keep Fallin' on My Head"

10. ___ will go down in history as my birthday.

○ A. October 13, 1967,
○ B. October 13 1967
○ C. October 13, 1967
○ D. October 13 1967,

11. ___ that alone!

○ A. Hey, Leave
○ B. Hey! Leave
○ C. Hey leave
○ D. Hey Leave

12. ___ is famous for its bullfights.

○ A. Madrid Spain
○ B. Madrid, Spain
○ C. Madrid Spain,
○ D. Madrid, Spain,

13. I ordered ___ from the menu.

○ A. eggs toast and coffee
○ B. eggs, toast, and coffee
○ C. eggs, toast and coffee
○ D. eggs, toast, and coffee,

14. Before he left, he said, "Don't give up the ___

○ A. fight."
○ B. fight"
○ C. fight".
○ D. fight,"

15. He signed the guest book ___ .

○ A. H L Chase
○ B. H L. Chase
○ C. H. L. Chase
○ D. H. L Chase

REFERENCE GUIDE

Grammar Rules

SENTENCES

Grammar 1. Definition of a sentence

A sentence is a group of words that expresses a complete thought. Every sentence must have a subject and a predicate. (See Grammar 3–6.) Every sentence begins with a capital letter and ends with a punctuation mark.

That leopard has already killed 400 people.

Is it still hungry?

Be careful!

Sometimes a sentence may have only one word. (See Grammar 5.)

Listen. *Hurry!*

Grammar 2. Kinds of sentences

There are four different kinds of sentences.

A *declarative sentence* makes a statement. A declarative sentence ends with a period.

A volcano in the Canary Islands is for sale.

An *interrogative sentence* asks a question. An interrogative sentence ends with a question mark.

Who would want to buy a volcano?

An *imperative sentence* gives a command. An imperative sentence ends with a period.

Show me the list of buyers.

An *exclamatory sentence* expresses excitement. An exclamatory sentence ends with an exclamation point.

They must be crazy!

Grammar 3. Subjects and predicates in declarative sentences

Every sentence has two main parts, the subject and the predicate. The subject names what the sentence is about. The predicate tells something about the subject.

In most declarative sentences, the subject is the first part. The predicate is the second part.

A famous sea captain *was often sick.*

He *suffered from seasickness.*

In some declarative sentences, the predicate is the first part. The subject is the second part.

Back and forth rolled *the captain's ship.*

Grammar 4. Subjects and predicates in interrogative sentences

Every interrogative sentence has a subject and a predicate. In some interrogative sentences, the subject is the first part. The predicate is the second part.

Who *solved the mystery?*

Which clue *was most important?*

In most interrogative sentences, part of the predicate comes before the subject. To find the subject and predicate, rearrange the words of the interrogative sentence. Use those words to make a declarative sentence. (The declarative sentence will not always sound natural, but it will help you.) The subject and predicate of the two sentences are the same.

Why did *the butler* *lie about it?*

The butler *did lie about it why?*

Grammar 5. Subjects and predicates in imperative sentences

Only the predicate of an imperative sentence is spoken or written. The subject of the sentence is understood. That subject is always **you.**

(You) Try an underhand serve.
(You) Please show me how to do it.

Grammar 6. Subjects and predicates in exclamatory sentences

Every exclamatory sentence has a subject and a predicate. In most exclamatory sentences, the subject is the first part. The predicate is the second part.

Kotzebue Sound, Alaska, is frozen over nearly all of the time!

In some exclamatory sentences, part of the predicate comes before the subject.

What terrible weather that city has!
(That city has what terrible weather!)

Grammar 7. Compound subjects in sentences

A sentence with a compound subject has two or more subjects with the same predicate.

***Jesse James and his brother Frank** were famous outlaws in the Old West.*

***Cole Younger, James Younger, and Robert Younger** were all members of the James gang.*

Grammar 8. Compound predicates in sentences

A sentence with a compound predicate has two or more predicates with the same subject.

*The postal workers **took in the tailless cat and named him Kojak.***

*Kojak **lives in the post office, catches mice, and earns a salary.***

Grammar 9. Compound sentences

A compound sentence is made up of two shorter sentences joined by a coordinating conjunction. (See Grammar 45.) A compound sentence has a subject and a predicate followed by another subject and another predicate.

G. David Howard set a record in 1978, and it remains unbroken.

Howard told jokes for more than 13 hours, but not all of them were funny.

NOUNS

Grammar 10. Definition of a noun

A noun is a word that names a person, a place, or a thing.

*That brave **man** crossed the **ocean** in a **rowboat.***

Grammar 11. Singular and plural forms of nouns

Almost every noun has two forms. The singular form names one person, place, or thing.

*Only one **worker** in that **factory** can name the secret **ingredient.***

The plural form names more than one person, place, or thing.

*Several **workers** in those two **factories** can name the secret **ingredients.***

Grammar 12. Spelling plural forms of nouns

For most nouns, add **s** to the singular form to make the plural form.

joke—jokes character—characters
cartoon—cartoons

If the singular form ends in **s, ss, sh, ch,** or **x,** add **es.**

bus—buses witch—witches
kiss—kisses fox—foxes
wish—wishes

If the singular form ends in a consonant and **y,** change the **y** to **i** and add **es.**

spy—spies discovery—discoveries
mystery—mysteries

If the singular form ends in **f,** usually change the **f** to **v** and add **es.** If the singular form ends in **fe,** usually change the **f** to **v** and add **s.** There are some important exceptions to these rules. Look in a dictionary if you are not sure of the correct plural form.

half—halves wife—wives
loaf—loaves knife—knives

Some exceptions:
roof—roofs chief—chiefs safe—safes

If the singular form ends in **o,** add **s** to some words and **es** to others. Look in a dictionary if you are not sure of the correct plural form.

studio—studios tomato—tomatoes
piano—pianos zero—zeroes

Some nouns change in other ways to make the plural form.

child—children *mouse—mice*
woman—women *goose—geese*

A few nouns have the same singular form and plural form.

sheep—sheep *deer—deer* *moose—moose*

Grammar 13. Proper nouns and common nouns

A proper noun is the special name of a particular person, place, or thing. Each word in a proper noun begins with a capital letter.

*Then **Max** stopped in **Junctionville** and ate a **Big Mac.***

A common noun is the name of any person, place, or thing.

*Then the **man** stopped in a small **town** and ate a **hamburger**.*

Grammar 14. Possessive nouns

The possessive form of a noun shows ownership. Usually the possessive form of a noun is made by adding an apostrophe and **s.** (See Punctuation 20.)

*A **piranha's** teeth are as sharp as razors.*

The possessive form of a plural noun that ends in **s** is made by adding only an apostrophe. (See Punctuation 20.)

*Nobody believed the **explorers'** story.*

Grammar 15. Nouns of address

A noun of address names the person being spoken to. One or two commas separate a noun of address from the rest of a sentence. (See Punctuation 9.)

*Where are you going, **Ricky?***

*I told you, **Lucy,** that I have a rehearsal tonight.*

Grammar 16. Appositive nouns

An appositive noun renames or identifies the noun that comes before it in a sentence. An appositive noun is usually part of a group of words. The whole group of words is called an appositive. One or two commas separate an appositive from the rest of a sentence. (See Punctuation 10.)

*A Ford was the preferred car of John Dillinger, **the famous gangster.***

*Even his sister, **the president of her own company,** would not hire him.*

VERBS

Grammar 17. Definition of a verb

A verb is a word that expresses action or being.

*The volcano **erupted** suddenly.*

*It **was** a terrific surprise.*

Almost all verbs have different forms to show differences in time.

*Sometimes puffs of smoke **rise** from the volcano.*

*A huge cloud of heavy gray smoke **rose** from it last week.*

Grammar 18. Action verbs

Most verbs are action verbs. An action verb expresses physical action or mental action.

*The committee members **banned** Donald Duck comic books.*

*They **disliked** the duck's behavior.*

Grammar 19. Linking verbs

Some verbs are linking verbs. A linking verb tells what the sentence subject is or is like. The most common linking verb is **be.** (See Grammar 23.)

*A black and white dog **became** a mail carrier in California.*

*The dog's name **was** Dorsey.*

Grammar 20. Verb phrases

A verb phrase is made up of two or more verbs that function together in a sentence. The final verb in a verb phrase is the main verb.

*The 13,000-pound bell **had disappeared.***

*Somebody **must have stolen** it.*

The verbs before the main verb in a verb phrase are helping verbs. The most common helping verbs are forms of **be** (**is, are, am, was, were**), forms of **have** (**has, have, had**), and forms of **do** (**does, do, did**). (See Grammar 23.)

*That radio station **is sponsoring** a contest.*

*The station **has** already **received** 45,217 postcards.*

Grammar 21. Agreement of verbs with nouns

Verbs that express continuing action or existence and verbs that express current action or existence are in the present tense. Almost all present-tense verbs have two different forms. These two different forms go with different sentence subjects. The verb in a sentence, or the first helping verb in a sentence, must agree with the most important word in the subject of that sentence.

One present-tense form of a verb agrees with singular nouns. This verb form ends with **s.**

A tick ***sucks*** *blood from larger animals.*

The other present-tense form of a verb agrees with plural nouns.

Ticks ***suck*** *blood from larger animals.*

Grammar 22. Agreement of verbs with compound subjects

The present-tense verb form that agrees with plural nouns also agrees with compound subjects. (See Grammar 7.)

Beth Obermeyer and her daughter Kristen ***hold*** *a record for long-distance tap dancing.*

Grammar 23. Forms of the verb *be*

The verb **be** has more forms than other verbs. **Be** has three present-tense forms: **is, are,** and **am. Is** agrees with singular nouns. **Are** agrees with plural nouns. **Am** agrees with the pronoun **I.**

Mary Lou Retton ***is*** *a famous gymnast.*

Many people ***are*** *her fans.*

I ***am*** *a pretty good gymnast, too.*

Most verbs have one past-tense form that tells about action or existence in the past. **Be** has two past-tense forms: **was** and **were. Was** agrees with singular noun subjects. **Were** agrees with plural noun subjects.

The argument ***was*** *noisy.*

Several neighbors ***were*** *very angry about it.*

Grammar 24. Irregular verbs

Usually the past-tense form of a verb ends in **d** or **ed.**

William Baxter ***invented*** *an important part of the Morse code.*

Some verbs change in other ways to form the past tense. These are called *irregular* verbs. Look in a dictionary if you are not sure of the correct past-tense form of a verb.

Samuel Morse ***took*** *all the credit.*

PRONOUNS

Grammar 25. Personal pronouns

A personal pronoun is a word that takes the place of one or more nouns.

Superman tried to enlist in the Army during World War II, but ***he*** *was found unfit to serve.*

Grammar 26. Subject forms and object forms of personal pronouns

Each personal pronoun has a subject form and an object form. These different forms are used in different ways in sentences. (The pronouns **it** and **you** are the same in the subject form and the object form.) These are the subject forms of personal pronouns: **I, you, he, she, it, we, they.** These are the object forms of personal pronouns: **me, you, him, her, it, us, them.**

He *saw through a wall and read the wrong eye chart.*

The army did not accept ***him.***

Grammar 27. Antecedents of pronouns

A personal pronoun refers to the noun it replaces. That noun is the antecedent of the pronoun.

Roy Rogers *became famous in movies.* ***He*** *was usually accompanied by his horse, Trigger, and his dog, Bullet.*

If a personal pronoun takes the place of two or more nouns, those nouns together are the antecedent of the pronoun.

Roy Rogers and Dale Evans *often worked together.* ***They*** *made dozens of movies.*

Grammar 28. Subject-verb agreement with personal pronouns

The present-tense verb form that agrees with singular nouns also agrees with the pronoun subjects **he, she,** and **it.**

She ***tests*** *new planes.*

The present-tense verb form that agrees with plural nouns also agrees with the pronoun subjects **I, you, we,** and **they.**

They ***test*** *new planes.*

Grammar 29. Indefinite pronouns

A word that refers to a general group but does not have a specific antecedent is an indefinite pronoun.

__Nobody__ can be right about __everything.__

One common indefinite pronoun, **no one,** is written as two words.

Grammar 30. Subject-verb agreement with indefinite pronouns

The present-tense verb form that agrees with singular nouns also agrees with most indefinite pronouns.

Almost everyone __remembers__ the Alamo.
No one __knows__ exactly what happened there.
Of the accounts written of the battle, several __claim__ to be factual.

Grammar 31. Possessive pronouns

A personal pronoun that shows ownership is a possessive pronoun.
These possessive pronouns are used before nouns in sentences: **my, your, his, her, its, our, their.**

Why are __my__ gym shoes in __your__ locker?

These possessive pronouns stand alone in sentences: **mine, yours, his, hers, its, ours, theirs.**

Are these gym shoes __mine,__ or are they __yours?__

Unlike possessive nouns, possessive pronouns are not written with apostrophes.

Grammar 32. Reflexive pronouns

A pronoun that refers back to a noun or pronoun in the same sentence is a reflexive pronoun. These words are reflexive pronouns: **myself, yourself, himself, herself, itself, ourselves, yourselves, themselves.**

The witness had been talking to __himself.__
You should have bought __yourself__ a ticket.

Grammar 33. Demonstrative pronouns

A word that points out one or more people or things is a demonstrative pronoun. These four words can be demonstrative pronouns: **this, that, these,** and **those.**

__These__ are the funniest cartoons.
Nobody laughed at __those.__

If the word **this, that, these,** or **those** is followed by a noun, the word is not a demonstrative pronoun. (See Grammar 34.)

ADJECTIVES

Grammar 34. Definition of an adjective

A word that adds to the meaning of a noun or pronoun is an adjective. Adjectives usually tell what kind, which one, or how many.

__Those exhausted__ men have been playing tennis for __nine__ hours.

Adjectives that tell what kind can sometimes stand alone.

They were __exhausted.__

Adjectives that tell which one or how many always come before nouns.

__Both__ players have used __several__ rackets.

Grammar 35. The adjectives *a* and *an*

The adjectives **a** and **an** are usually called *indefinite articles.* (The adjective **the** is usually called a *definite article.*) **A** is used before words that begin with consonants or with a "yew" sound.

__A__ penguin cannot fly.
Cooking is __a__ useful activity.

An is used before words that begin with vowels or with an unsounded **h.**

__An__ ostrich cannot fly.
Brutus is __an__ honorable man.

Grammar 36. Predicate adjectives

An adjective that comes after a linking verb and adds to the meaning of the subject noun or pronoun is a predicate adjective.

Maria Spelterina must have been __brave.__
Her tightrope walks across Niagara Falls were __dangerous.__

Grammar 37. Proper adjectives

An adjective that is formed from a proper noun is a proper adjective. Each word in a proper adjective begins with a capital letter.

The __American__ dollar is worth less than the __British__ pound.
The new __Spielberg__ film is great!

Grammar 38. Comparative and superlative forms of adjectives

Adjectives can be used to compare two or more people or things. When only two people or things are compared, use the comparative form of an adjective. To make the comparative form, add **er** to adjectives with one syllable and many adjectives with two syllables. Use **more** (or **less**) before some adjectives with two syllables and all adjectives with more than two syllables. Look in a dictionary if you are not sure of the correct comparative form of an adjective.

Buster Keaton was ***funnier*** *than Charlie Chaplin.*

Buster Keaton was ***more amusing*** *than Charlie Chaplin.*

When more than two people or things are compared, use the superlative form of an adjective. To make the superlative form, add **est** to adjectives with one syllable and many adjectives with two syllables. Use **most** (or **least**) before some adjectives with two syllables and all adjectives with more than two syllables. Look in a dictionary if you are not sure of the correct superlative form of an adjective.

Buster Keaton was the ***funniest*** *movie actor who ever lived.*

Buster Keaton was the ***most amusing*** *movie actor who ever lived.*

The comparative and superlative forms of the adjective **good** are **better** and **best.**

Buster Keaton was a ***better*** *actor than Charlie Chaplin.*

Buster Keaton was the ***best*** *movie actor who ever lived.*

The comparative and superlative forms of the adjective **bad** are **worse** and **worst.**

The Revenge of the Killer Tomatoes was a ***worse*** *movie than The Fly.*

The Revenge of the Killer Tomatoes was probably the ***worst*** *movie ever made.*

ADVERBS

Grammar 39. Definition of an adverb

A word that adds to the meaning of a verb or verb phrase is an adverb. Adverbs usually tell where, when, how, or how often.

The rodeo rider ***bravely*** *mounted the mustang* ***again.***

Grammar 40. Comparative and superlative forms of adverbs

Adverbs can be used to compare the actions of two or more people or things.

When only two people or things are compared, use the comparative form of an adverb. To make the comparative form, usually use **more** (or **less**) before the adverb. Add **er** to a few short adverbs.

Polly speaks ***more clearly*** *than that other parrot.*

Polly can fly ***higher*** *than that other parrot.*

When more than two people or things are compared, use the superlative form of an adverb. To make the superlative form, usually use **most** (or **least**) before the adverb. Add **est** to a few short adverbs.

Of all those parrots, Polly speaks ***most clearly.***

Of all those parrots, Polly can fly ***highest.***

The comparative and superlative forms of the adverb **well** are **better** and **best.**

That parrot behaved ***better*** *than your pet cat.*

Of all the unusual pets in the show, the parrot behaved ***best.***

The comparative and superlative forms of the adverb **badly** are **worse** and **worst.**

Your pet monkey behaved ***worse*** *than that parrot.*

Of all the unusual pets in the show, your cat behaved ***worst.***

Grammar 41. Using adjectives and adverbs

Use an adjective to add to the meaning of a noun or a pronoun.

The ***proud*** *actor accepted the prize.*

Use an adverb to add to the meaning of a verb or a verb phrase. Many (but not all) adverbs end in **ly.**

The actor accepted the prize ***proudly.***

Grammar 42. The adverb *not*

The adverb **not** changes the meaning of the verb or verb phrase in a sentence.

The soldiers in the fort would ***not*** *surrender.*

Help did ***not*** *arrive in time.*

Grammar 43. Avoiding double negatives

The adverb **not** is a negative word. Other common negative words are **no, never, no one, nobody, nothing, nowhere, hardly, barely,** and **scarcely.** Use only one negative word to make a sentence mean **no** or **not.**

No one *ever understands how I feel.*

My friends ***never*** *understand how I feel.*

Hardly *anyone understands how I feel.*

Grammar 44. Adverbs used as intensifiers

Certain adverbs add to the meaning of adjectives or other adverbs. These special adverbs are sometimes called *intensifiers.*

One ***terribly*** *nosy neighbor heard the whole conversation.*

Very *nervously, she told the police all about it.*

CONJUNCTIONS

Grammar 45. Coordinating conjunctions

A word used to join two equal parts of a sentence is a coordinating conjunction. The most common coordinating conjunctions are **and, but,** and **or.**

Many people have driven across the country, ***but*** *these two men did it the hard way.*

Charles Creighton ***and*** *James Hargis drove across the country* ***and*** *back again.*

They never stopped the engine ***or*** *took the car out of reverse gear.*

Grammar 46. Subordinating conjunctions and complex sentences

A word used to begin an adverb clause is a subordinating conjunction. The most common subordinating conjunctions are listed below.

after	before	though	when
although	if	unless	whenever
because	since	until	while

An adverb clause is a group of words that has a subject and a predicate but that cannot stand alone as a sentence. An adverb clause functions like an adverb. It tells when, where, how, or why. An adverb clause usually comes at the end or at the beginning of a sentence. (See Punctuation 8.) A sentence formed from an adverb clause (which cannot stand alone) and a main clause (which can stand alone) is called a *complex sentence.*

Otto E. Funk played his violin ***while he walked from New York City to San Francisco.***

When he finished his musical journey, *both his feet and his hands were tired.*

Whenever it is threatened, *an opossum plays dead.*

It can be poked, picked up, and even rolled over ***while it remains completely rigid.***

INTERJECTIONS

Grammar 47. Definition of an interjection

A word that simply expresses emotion is an interjection. A comma or an exclamation point separates an interjection from the rest of a sentence. (See Punctuation 11.)

Oh, *now it makes sense.*

Wow! *That's terrific news!*

PREPOSITIONS

Grammar 48. Definition of a preposition

A word that shows the relationship of a noun or pronoun to some other word in a sentence is a preposition. The most common prepositions are listed below.

about	below	in	to
above	beneath	into	toward
across	beside	like	under
after	between	of	until
against	beyond	off	up
along	by	on	upon
among	down	over	with
around	during	past	within
at	except	since	without
before	for	through	
behind	from	throughout	

Grammar 49. Prepositional phrases

A preposition must be followed by a noun or a pronoun. The preposition and the noun or pronoun that follows it form a prepositional phrase.

A new record ***for sit-ups*** *was set* ***by Dr. David G. Jones.***

His family and friends were very proud ***of him.***

Often, other words come between the preposition and the noun or pronoun. Those words are also part of the prepositional phrase.

He set a new record ***for consecutive straight-legged sit-ups.***

Grammar 50. Objects of prepositions

A preposition must be followed by a noun or a pronoun. That noun or pronoun is the object of the preposition.

One of the main ***characters*** *of* ***<u>Star Trek</u>*** *didn't appear until the second* ***season.***

Grammar 51. Personal pronouns in prepositional phrases

A personal pronoun that is the object of a preposition should be in the object form. These are object-form pronouns: **me, you, him, her, it, us, them.**

The other presents for ***her*** *are still on the table.*
The most interesting present is from ***me.***

Grammar 52. Prepositional phrases used as adjectives

Some prepositional phrases are used as adjectives. They add to the meaning of a noun or pronoun in a sentence.

The Caribbean island ***of Martinique*** *is a department* ***of the French government.***

Grammar 53. Prepositional phrases used as adverbs

Some prepositional phrases are used as adverbs. They add to the meaning of the verb or verb phrase in a sentence.

In 1763, *Napoleon Bonaparte's wife, Josephine, was born* ***on Martinique.***

SENTENCE PARTS

Grammar 54. Simple subjects

The most important noun or pronoun in the subject of a sentence is the simple subject of that sentence. The object of a preposition cannot be the simple subject of a sentence.

A 27-year-old ***man*** *from Oklahoma swam the entire length of the Mississippi River.*
He *spent a total of 742 hours in the river.*

Grammar 55. Simple predicates

The verb or verb phrase of a sentence is the simple predicate of that sentence.

Actor W. C. Fields ***may have had*** *700 separate savings accounts.*
Fields ***used*** *a different name for each account.*

Grammar 56. Direct objects

A word that tells who or what receives the action of a verb is the direct object of the verb. A direct object must be a noun or a pronoun. A personal pronoun that is a direct object should be in the object form. These are object-form pronouns: **me, you, him, her, it, us, them.**

The first aspirin tablets contained ***heroin.***
A German company sold ***them*** *for 12 years.*

Grammar 57. Indirect objects

A word that tells to whom (or what) or for whom (or what) something is done is the indirect object of the verb expressing the action. An indirect object comes before a direct object and is not part of a prepositional phrase. An indirect object must be a noun or a pronoun. A personal pronoun that is a direct object should be in the object form. These are object-form pronouns: **me, you, him, her, it, us, them.**

Professor Sommers gave his ***students*** *the same lecture every year.*
He told ***them*** *a familiar story.*

Grammar 58. Predicate nominatives

A word that follows a linking verb and renames the sentence subject is the predicate nominative of a sentence. A predicate nominative must be a noun or a pronoun. A personal pronoun that is a predicate nominative should be in the subject form. These are subject-form pronouns: **I, you, he, she, it, we, they.**

The best candidate was ***Andrea.***
In my opinion, the winner should have been ***she.***

Capitalization Rules

Capitalization 1. First word in a sentence

Begin the first word in every sentence with a capital letter.

__Who__ won the eating contest?
__That__ man ate 17 bananas in two minutes.

Capitalization 2. Personal pronoun *I*

Write the pronoun **I** with a capital letter.

At the last possible minute, __I__ changed my mind.

Capitalization 3. Names and initials of people

Almost always, begin each part of a person's name with a capital letter.

Toby Ohara Rosie Delancy
Sue Ellen Macmillan

Some names have more than one capital letter. Other names have parts that are not capitalized. Check the correct way to write each person's name. (Look in a reference book, or ask the person.)

Tim O'Hara Tony de la Cruz
Jeannie McIntyre

Use a capital letter to write an initial that is part of a person's name.

B. J. Gallardo J. Kelly Hunt
John F. Kennedy

Capitalization 4. Titles of people

Begin the title before a person's name with a capital letter.

***Mr.** Sam Yee **Captain** Cook*
***Dr.** Watson **Governor** Maxine Smart*

Do not use a capital letter if this kind of word is not used before a person's name.

Did you call the __doctor?__
Who will be our state's next __governor?__

Capitalization 5. Names of relatives

A word like **grandma** or **uncle** may be used as a person's name or as part of a person's name. Begin this kind of word with a capital letter.

Only __Dad__ and __Aunt Ellie__ understand it.

Usually, if a possessive pronoun comes before a word like **grandma** or **uncle,** do not begin that word with a capital letter.

Only __my dad__ and __my aunt__ understand it.

Capitalization 6. Names of days

Begin the name of a day with a capital letter.

Most people don't have to work on __Saturday__ or __Sunday.__

Capitalization 7. Names of months

Begin the name of a month with a capital letter.

At the equator, the hottest months are __March__ and __September.__

Capitalization 8. Names of holidays

Begin each important word in the name of a holiday with a capital letter. Words like **the** and **of** do not begin with capital letters.

They usually have a picnic on the __Fourth of July__ and a fancy dinner party on __Thanksgiving.__

Capitalization 9. Names of streets and highways

Begin each word in the name of a street or highway with a capital letter.

Why is __Lombard Street__ known as the most crooked road in the world?

Capitalization 10. Names of cities and towns

Begin each word in the name of a city or town with a capital letter.

In 1957, the Dodgers moved from __Brooklyn__ to __Los Angeles.__

Capitalization 11. Names of states, countries, and continents

Begin each word in the name of a state, country, or continent with a capital letter.

The story was set in __Nevada,__ but they shot the film in __Mexico.__
There are very high mountain peaks in __Antarctica.__

Capitalization 12. Names of mountains and bodies of water

Begin each word in the name of a mountain, river, lake, or ocean with a capital letter.

*Amelia Earhart's plane was lost somewhere over the **Pacific Ocean.***

Capitalization 13. Abbreviations

If the word would begin with a capital letter, begin the abbreviation with a capital letter.

*On the scrap of paper, the victim had written, "**Wed.—Dr.** Lau."*

Capitalization 14. Titles of works

Use a capital letter to begin the first word, the last word, and every main word in the title of a work. The words **the, a,** and **an** do not begin with capital letters except at the beginning of a title. Coordinating conjunctions and prepositions also do not begin with capital letters. (See Grammar 45 and Grammar 48.)

*Archie and Edith were the main characters in the television series **<u>All in the Family</u>.***

Capitalization 15. Other proper nouns

Begin each major word in a proper noun with a capital letter. A proper noun is the special name of a particular person, place, or thing. (See Grammar 13.) Usually, the words **the, a,** and **an,** coordinating conjunctions, and prepositions do not begin with capital letters. (See Grammar 45 and Grammar 48.)

*Jerry rushed to the **Burger King** and ordered three **Whoppers.***

Capitalization 16. Proper adjectives

Begin each word in a proper adjective with a capital letter. A proper adjective is an adjective that is formed from a proper noun. (See Grammar 37.)

*That **American** author writes about **English** detectives.*

*She loves **Alfred Hitchcock** movies.*

Capitalization 17. Direct quotations

Begin the first word in a direct quotation with a capital letter. (See Punctuation 14–16.)

*Dr. Pavlik said, **"There** are simply no teeth in the denture law."*

If the words that tell who is speaking come in the middle of a quoted sentence, do not begin the second part of the quotation with a capital letter.

***"There** are simply no teeth," said Dr. Pavlik, **"in** the denture law."*

Capitalization 18. Greetings and closings in letters

Begin the first word in the greeting of a letter with a capital letter.

***Dear** Mr. Lincoln:* ***Dear** Uncle Abe,*

Begin the first or only word in the closing of a letter with a capital letter.

***Sincerely** yours,* ***Very** truly yours,*
Love,

Capitalization 19. Outlines

In an outline, begin the first word of each heading with a capital letter.

II. Houses by mail order
A. First sold by Sears, Roebuck in 1903
1. Build-it-yourself kits
2. Included all materials and instructions
B. Other companies now in business

In an outline, use capital Roman numerals to label main ideas. Use capital letters to label supporting ideas. For ideas under supporting ideas, use Arabic numerals. For details, use small letters. Use a period after each Roman numeral, capital letter, Arabic numeral, or small letter.

I. Miner George Warren
A. Risked his share of Copper Queen mine in bet
1. Bet on race against George Atkins
a. Warren on foot
b. Atkins on horseback
2. Lost property worth $20 million

Punctuation Rules

Punctuation 1. Periods, question marks, and exclamation points at the ends of sentences

Use a period, a question mark, or an exclamation point at the end of every sentence. Do not use more than one of these marks at the end of a sentence. For example, do not use both a question mark and an exclamation point, or do not use two exclamation points.

Use a period at the end of a declarative sentence (a sentence that makes a statement).

A hockey player must be able to skate backward at top speed.

Also use a period at the end of an imperative sentence (a sentence that gives a command).

Keep your eye on the puck.

Use a question mark at the end of an interrogative sentence (a sentence that asks a question).

Who is the goalie for their team?

Use an exclamation point at the end of an exclamatory sentence (a sentence that expresses excitement).

That was a terrific block!

Punctuation 2. Periods with abbreviations

Use a period at the end of each part of an abbreviation.

Most titles used before people's names are abbreviations. These abbreviations may be used in formal writing. (**Miss** is not an abbreviation and does not end with a period.)

Dr. *Blackwell* ***Mr.*** *Bill Tilden*
Ms. *Maureen Connolly*

Most other abbreviations may be used in addresses, notes, and informal writing. They should not be used in formal writing.

Lake View ***Blvd.*** ***Mon.*** *and* ***Thurs.***
Fifth ***Ave.*** ***Dec.*** *24*

Do not use periods in the abbreviations of names of government agencies, labor unions, and certain other organizations.

Tomorrow night ***CBS*** *will broadcast a special program about the* ***FBI.***

Do not use periods after two-letter state abbreviations in addresses. This special kind of abbreviation has two capital letters and no period. Use these abbreviations only in addresses.

Their new address is 1887 West Third Street, Los Angeles, ***CA*** *90048.*

Punctuation 3. Periods after initials

Use a period after an initial that is part of a person's name.

Chester ***A.*** *Arthur* ***C. C.*** *Pyle*
Susan ***B.*** *Anthony*

Punctuation 4. Commas in dates

Use a comma between the number of the day and the number of the year in a date.

Hank Aaron hit his record-breaking home run on ***April 8, 1974.***

If the date does not come at the end of a sentence, use another comma after the number of the year.

April 8, 1974, *was an exciting day for Hank Aaron's fans.*

Do not use a comma in a date that has only the name of a month and the number of a year.

Aaron hit his final home run in ***July 1976.***

Do not use a comma in a date that has only the name of a month and the number of a day.

April 8 *is the anniversary of Aaron's record-breaking home run.*

Punctuation 5. Commas in place names

Use a comma between the name of a city or town and the name of a state or country.

The world's largest chocolate factory is in ***Hershey, Pennsylvania.***

If the two names do not come at the end of a sentence, use another comma after the name of the state or country.

Hershey, Pennsylvania, *is the home of the world's largest chocolate factory.*

Punctuation 6. Commas in compound sentences

Use a comma before the conjunction—**and, but,** or **or**—in a compound sentence. (See Grammar 9 and Grammar 45.)

Eighteen people tried, ***but*** *no one succeeded.*

Punctuation 7. Commas in series

Three or more words or groups of words used the same way in a sentence form a series. Use commas to separate the words or word groups in a series.

Jamie, Mitch, Kim, Lou, and Pablo *entered the contest.*

Each contestant ***swam one mile, bicycled two miles, and ran five miles.***

Punctuation 8. Commas after introductory phrases and clauses

Use a comma after a phrase that comes before the subject of a sentence. A phrase is a group of words that usually functions as an adjective or an adverb. One kind of phrase is a prepositional phrase. (See Grammar 49.)

In the old dresser, *Penny found the diamonds.*

If the entire predicate comes before the subject of the sentence, do not use a comma. (See Grammar 3.)

In the old dresser lay the diamonds.

Use a comma after an adverb clause at the beginning of a sentence. (See Grammar 46.)

When he was first named hockey's most valuable player, *Wayne Gretzky was only 18 years old.*

Punctuation 9. Commas with nouns of address

Use a comma after a noun of address at the beginning of a sentence. (See Grammar 15.)

Fernando, *that was a terrific pitch!*

Use a comma before a noun of address at the end of a sentence.

That was a terrific pitch, ***Fernando!***

If a noun of address comes in the middle of a sentence, use one comma before the noun and another comma after it.

That, ***Fernando,*** *was a terrific pitch!*

Punctuation 10. Commas with appositives

Use a comma before an appositive at the end of a sentence. (See Grammar 16.)

This costume was worn by George Reeves, ***Hollywood's first Superman.***

If an appositive comes in the middle of a sentence, use one comma before the appositive and another comma after it.

George Reeves, ***Hollywood's first Superman,*** *wore this costume.*

Punctuation 11. Commas or exclamation points with interjections

Usually, use a comma after an interjection. (See Grammar 47.)

Well, *we should probably think about it.*

Use an exclamation point after an interjection that expresses excitement.

Wow! *That's a terrific idea!*

Punctuation 12. Commas after greetings in friendly letters

Use a comma after the greeting in a friendly letter.

Dear John,   *Dear Uncle Theodore,*

Punctuation 13. Commas after closings in friendly letters and business letters

Use a comma after the closing in a letter.

Love,   *Yours sincerely,*

Punctuation 14. Quotation marks with direct quotations

A direct quotation tells the exact words a person said. Use quotation marks at the beginning and at the end of each part of a direct quotation.

"Look!" cried Tina. "That cat is smiling!"

"Of course," said Tom. "It's a Cheshire cat."

Punctuation 15. Commas with direct quotations

Usually, use a comma to separate the words of a direct quotation from the words that tell who is speaking. (See Punctuation 16.)

Jay asked, "Who won the game last night?"

"The Cubs won it," said Linda, "in 14 innings."

Punctuation 16. End punctuation with direct quotations

At the end of a direct quotation, use a period, a comma, a question mark, or an exclamation point before the closing quotation marks.

If the direct quotation makes a statement or gives a command at the end of a sentence, use a period.

Linda said, "The Cubs won last night's game."
Jay said, "Tell us about the game."

If the direct quotation makes a statement or gives a command before the end of a sentence, use a comma.

"The Cubs won last night's game," said Linda.
"Tell us about the game," Jay said.

If the direct quotation asks a question, use a question mark.

"Was it an exciting game?" asked Jay.

If the direct quotation expresses excitement, use an exclamation point.

Linda yelled, "It was great!"

Punctuation 17. Quotation marks with titles of works

Use quotation marks around the title of a story, poem, song, essay, or chapter.

"Happy Birthday to You" *is the most popular song in the world.*

If a period or a comma comes after the title, put the period or comma inside the closing quotation mark.

The most popular song in the world is ***"Happy Birthday to You."***

Punctuation 18. Underlines with titles of works

Underline the title of a book, play, magazine, movie, television series, or newspaper.

One of the best movies about baseball was ***The Natural.***

Punctuation 19. Apostrophes in contractions

Use an apostrophe in place of the missing letter or letters in a contraction.

is not—isn't *Mel is—Mel's* *I will—I'll*

Punctuation 20. Apostrophes in possessive nouns

Use an apostrophe and **s** to write the possessive form of a singular noun. (See Grammar 14.)

This cage belongs to one bird. It is the ***bird's*** *cage.*
This cage belongs to Tweeter. It is ***Tweeter's*** *cage.*

Use only an apostrophe to write the possessive form of a plural noun that ends in **s.**

This is a club for boys. It is a ***boys'*** *club.*

Use an apostrophe and **s** to write the possessive form of a plural noun that does not end in **s.**

This is a club for men. It is a ***men's*** *club.*

Punctuation 21. Colons after greetings in business letters

Use a colon after the greeting in a business letter.

Dear Mrs. Huan: *Dear Sir or Madam:*
Dear Senator Rayburn:

Punctuation 22. Colons in expressions of time

When you use numerals to write time, use a colon between the hour and the minutes.

5:45 P.M. *9:00 A.M.* *12:17 P.M.*

Punctuation 23. Hyphens in numbers and fractions

Use a hyphen in a compound number from twenty-one to ninety-nine.

thirty-seven *fifty-eight* *seventy-three*

Use a hyphen in a fraction.

one-quarter *two-thirds* *seven-eighths*